To Rick

Changing Looks —
Changing Lives

All the best!
love

ELEANOR FULCHER

Changing Looks — Changing Lives

 A MEMOIR

Changing Looks - Changing Lives: a memoir
Published by The Hilborn Group Ltd.
Editorial & Communications Services
Box 86, Station C, Toronto ON, M6J 3M7 Canada

Book design and composition by Susan Hood Design
Article by George Gamester used with permission of The
Toronto Star

Library and Archives Canada Cataloguing in Publication
Fulcher, Eleanor, author
Changing looks - changing lives : a memoir / Eleanor Fulcher.
Issued in print and electronic formats.
ISBN 978-1-927375-24-2 (pbk.)
978-1-927375-25-9 (kindle)
1. Fulcher, Eleanor. 2. E. Fulcher Group--Employees--Bi-
ography. 3. Businesswomen--Canada--Biography. 4. Mod-
eling agencies--Canada.   5. Entrepreneurship--Canada.
I. Title.
HD9999.M642F85 2015 659.1'52 C2015-901831-5
C2015-901832-3

THIS BOOK IS DEDICATED TO EVERYONE WHO
PARTICIPATED, ENJOYED AND BENEFITTED FROM
THE ELEANOR FULCHER SCHOOL AND AGENCY.
WE HAD GREAT FUN, DIDN'T WE!

and also . . .

TO THE MEMORY OF MY GRANDMOTHERS,
TELLA FULCHER AND CHARLOTTE ROOKE,
BOTH INCREDIBLY STRONG WOMEN WHO
SOMEHOW MANAGED TO RAISE LARGE FAMILIES
ON VERY LITTLE MONEY AND WITH VERY LITTLE
HELP. THEY WERE BOTH AMAZINGLY RESOURCEFUL.
I LIKE TO THINK SOME OF MY BETTER QUALITIES —
PERSEVERANCE, DEDICATION, BLIND FAITH —
CAME FROM THEM — MY GUARDIAN ANGELS!

CONTENTS

Preface

I wanted to write this book for a few reasons. I think my story is part of an especially interesting time in women's history. I was born in 1934. In the '30s, '40s and early '50s, men had career opportunities and advantages most women could never enjoy. The traditional jobs for women were secretary, teacher, stewardess or nurse. Education and skill development for these jobs were just steppingstones to the ultimate goal of getting married and having children. Advertisements showed housewives overjoyed at getting a Hoover vacuum for Christmas or smiling gratefully at their new refrigerator. The message was, if you want to be happy and fulfilled, be a good wife, mother and housekeeper. If, God help you, you couldn't find a suitable husband, you'd be labelled a spinster or old maid by the time you were 25!

I was surrounded by that attitude. It was ingrained in all females from an early age. But one day I had an epiphany that changed my life. I was 17 and working as a secretary at Lever Brothers in Toronto,

Ontario, looking at all these bright, energetic women typing all day in the secretarial pool. It hit me: That's me in ten years! Was that all life had in store for me?

I decided there had to be a lot more out there for Eleanor Fulcher, so I quit my job that same day — and it was a great job. I spent the next eight years experiencing the ups and downs in the beauty, modelling and secretarial fields, and then, against all odds, I started my own business. The year was 1960. The time was right. The Eleanor Fulcher School and Agency grew in leaps and bounds to become the biggest in Canada. Building my business wasn't easy, but it was exciting and challenging. Today I feel like I've lived my life the way I wanted to, not the way someone or society expected me to.

Times have changed and women have many more opportunities, but older women still have to fight against the image society has of us. When I'm with my contemporaries, I look around the room and see beautiful, strong women, smartly dressed, sharp. None of us is ready to give up and let ourselves age and look "old." I'm healthy and happy and I take care of myself. In 2012, I celebrated 50 years of marriage to my husband, Bruno Arnold. (And they said it wouldn't last!) We have dear friends and a great family — our daughter Angela, our son Marcus and his wife Lori, and our grandchildren Joseph, Vittoria, Peyton and Madison. Life is good.

So with this book, I'm volunteering to be the poster child for my generation. I'm alive and kicking and feeling great, getting up at 6:20 a.m., exercising, doing my hair and makeup, eating well, doing the *Globe and Mail* bridge column and crossword puzzle, and dressing for whatever the day throws at me. At 9:30 a.m. I am "ready for anything"!

So let's rewind.

CHAPTER 1

My Roots and Family

The Fulcher Clan

My paternal grandfather was a brickmaker named Frederick Fulcher, born in Burton-Upon-Trent, England, on September 12, 1880. Frederick was one of seven children. His childhood was very rough. He was separated from his entire family while quite young and sent to a workhouse, and later was put on a ship to Canada to work on a farm as one of the Barnardo Boys, as these young waifs were called. I don't know anything about his life in those early years. At one point he joined the 48th Highlanders and fought at Vimy Ridge. He married my grandmother Tella Hansen (or Hausen, as it's spelled on some documents) on December 1, 1908.

Tella was born December 23, 1885, in Mosjøen, Norway, and came to Canada in 1907. I loved and admired my grandmother Fulcher. I was 15 when she died on February 4, 1949, and felt her loss very deeply — and still do.

3

My brother Freddy and me with our grandparents Tella Fulcher (née Hansen) and Frederick Fulcher

Frederick and Tella had six children, the eldest being my father, also named Frederick (Fred). My dad was born August 27, 1909. He lived until he was 77, when he died of prostate cancer. The 1911 census of Canada shows Frederick, Tella and my father, Fred, living at 158 Sackville Street, Toronto.

My father was a labourer, an incredibly strong man. My brother, also named Fred (Freddy), worked with him part time during the summers, hauling ice to refrigerators, and even though my brother is also very strong, he told me once that he watched Dad pick up a 50-pound brick of ice and fling it over his shoulder like it weighed no more than three pounds. Fred tried to copy him and could barely lift it! My dad was very quiet and laid back. He had a moustache and a bit of the Clark Gable look. Women thought he was very handsome.

Left to right: Aunt Mabel, Grandma Fulcher,
Aunt Gladys, Aunt Edna and Uncle Bobby

My dad's home life growing up was difficult. My grandfather Fulcher abused both my grandmother and my dad's younger brother Charlie. Maybe he also mistreated the three daughters — Gladys, Edna and Mabel — and the youngest brother, Bobby, whom I had a crush on. I don't know. My aunts always said their father was mean. He didn't allow them to finish school, didn't allow them to do anything. He didn't pick on my dad because he knew he would lose. But Charlie was a small, skinny guy and no match for his dad's wrath. My dad helped Charlie run away from home one night when he couldn't take it anymore.

I used to judge my grandfather Fulcher harshly, and I still don't excuse his actions, but now that I know about his very difficult childhood and younger years, I can understand him a bit better.

Losing his parents, living a miserable existence as a child in a work-house, ripped from his brothers and sisters and sent to Canada to work in the fields, serving with the 48th Highlanders during World War I — he did not have an easy life. Who knows what happens to the mind and the spirit when you have to endure so much without any support?

When he was just 14 years old, my dad's brother Charlie, having run away, ended up in the United States. He started out in Florida and at some point spent some time in Cuba. He became a horse trainer and travelled throughout the States with the horses. He'd carry a carrot in his pocket so the horses would follow him. One time a horse van ran over him and he was in the hospital for a year. They saved his ankle but it was deformed after that and he walked with a limp. Because of Uncle Charlie I have a large U.S. family, including my younger cousin, Gay, Charlie's daughter, whom I'm especially close to. Gay has three daughters: Cheryl, Pam and Lori. Lori came to live with me for a year when she was 18. She took my modelling course and went on to become a full-time model, travel-

My second cousin Lori

ling to exotic places. She even got interested in my spa, and when she went back to her home in New York she worked between modelling and the spa industry. She's like a second daughter to me.

One day my dad and I were driving along Highway 401 east to Albert College in Belleville to visit my daughter, Angela, where she was enrolled, when we noticed a sign for the town of Cobourg. My dad very casually said, "Oh, Cobourg. We lived there for a year."

I said, "What? When?"

"It was when Mom left Dad. She took us five kids. She was pregnant. Had no money." My dad told me they lived there for about a year. His mom took in laundry to pay for food, but she just couldn't manage — no welfare, no employment insurance, no support of any kind. She had no choice but to go back to my grandfather. I found out recently from my cousin Sharon that my grandmother gave birth to my Aunt Mabel while she was in Cobourg. I can't imagine the hardships my grandmother Fulcher must have endured. I guess she came from Norway thinking she would find a better life.

I adored her. She adored me too and I really felt her love. Her English wasn't good but she had a heart as big as the prairies. Every Sunday we went to her house for dinner. She made a magnificent roast beef that had the most unbelievably delicious aroma. I had almost forgotten about those wonderful, growing-up Sunday dinners until one day Bruno and I were in Switzerland and we walked into a restaurant and I smelled that same wonderful aroma. What memories came rushing back! My grandmother would seat everyone around a couple of tables pushed together. Most of her six children were married with kids of their own, so there were about 14 of us at the table. She'd be in the kitchen, working; she'd never sit down with us. They had this old woodstove that she cooked everything on. She made her own bread — everything was from scratch of course — and there was enough food to feed an army. She waited on us hand and foot and was so happy to see everyone eating and enjoying one another, hovering over us to make sure we had enough to eat. When I think back on it, we should have forced her kicking and screaming to come and sit down with us. But she didn't want to — she wanted to wait on us and that was her way. This is when she was happy, when we were all together. Her daughter, my Aunt Gladys, played the piano by ear and I loved to sing along. The men played crokinole or cards. Sometimes we all stood around the piano and sang the popular songs of the day. I knew the words to all of them.

I used to stay with my grandmother Tella for a week during my summer vacation. For many years they had an outhouse, for those of you who remember. She had somehow managed to buy this house, which is important for a European. But even in those days you needed to have a good down payment, so I don't know how she did it. Maybe she was skimming a little here and there and keeping it safe in a cookie jar. If so, good for her.

My grandfather was a hard worker, a labourer. But money was always tight. Even though my grandmother Tella couldn't afford anything, she took me out shopping. When we were out together, she'd take my hand and we'd go up to the bakery window and look at all the tarts and goodies and she'd say, "Which one would you like, Eleanor? You can have any one you want." "I'd like a chocolate éclair," I'd say, and we'd go in the bakery with all its wonderful aromas and choices, and she'd have the baker wrap up my selection in a little box tied with a pretty ribbon. We'd get home and she would watch me unwrap the box and eat my treat. It never occurred to me that she could only afford one treat; that she might have liked one too, or at least that I could have shared mine! Other times, we'd go to the market and she'd say, "Let's get you an apple today. Any apple you want." And I'd pick out the best, shiniest apple — I was only seven or eight at the time, but that was exciting. But what is apparent to me now is that all she could afford was the one apple. I could cry thinking about it now. She was an incredible woman, a warm, giving person who deserved a lot more than she got out of life.

I carry a lot of remorse — what I could have or should have done had I been more aware, more mature. And the way she died! It was stomach cancer. I remember walking into her house one day and I heard a dog howling. I said to my Aunt Edna, "I didn't know you had a dog." It wasn't a dog. It was my grandmother Tella, crying out in pain and suffering, dying of stomach cancer with no relief from morphine or any drugs to ease her suffering. I never got to tell her how much I loved her. I miss her still.

The Rookes

On my mother's side there was my grandfather Isaac Rooke, born in 1875. He was a house painter who died at age 54 from, they thought, inhaling too many paint fumes.

My grandmother's name was Charlotte but we called her Maw. She had one front tooth. In those days the dentists didn't bother fixing your teeth. It was cheaper to just pull them and give you false teeth. And of course there was no such thing as freezing. The story behind her having just one tooth is that one day, the dentist decided to pull out all her teeth and give her false teeth, but when he was about to take out the last tooth she was in such pain that she shoved him away and ran out, and vowed never to go to a dentist again. And she never did. I can understand that. When I was a kid the dentist would keep drilling your tooth, with no freezing, until he hit a nerve, and you'd scream in pain. Then they'd start filling.

Maw married Isaac when she was only 17. He was quite well off and owned a chain of variety stores. But unfortunately, he got hooked on horse racing and little by little he lost everything due to

Left, my mom, Muriel Rooke, at 18 months
old, and her sister Helen at 2 ½ years old

his bad wagers and ended up a house painter. This addiction to the races showed up in one of his sons, my Uncle Norman, who used to go to the racetrack every day.

Isaac and Charlotte had six children, one of whom was my mother, Muriel Elizabeth Rooke, along with her sister, Helen, and four boys — Raymond, Norman, Bernie and Melville. Around 1950, my brother Fred, Bernie and Melville formed a singing trio, The Three Rookies. On both sides of the family, the Rookes and the Fulchers, there's musical talent. My brother was only about 16 and my uncles were older, maybe 20 or 22, and they all had terrific voices and all played the guitar. They were first runners-up in the Ken Soble National Talent Contest. The Three Rookies played a lot of gigs at schools and bars and social gatherings and they were doing well and even making a little money. But then, through some mis-understanding or other interests, they broke up. I think if they had stayed together they could have become famous. There were a num-ber of popular men's singing groups at the time: the Ink Spots, the Mills Brothers, the Jersey Boys, the Platters. Trios were especially popular at that time and The Three Rookies were all good-looking, talented guys. They actually made a recording of "The Anniversary Song" and "P.S. I Love You," which I still listen to now and then and wonder what might have happened if they'd stayed together.

After my grandfather Isaac Rooke died, Maw had to scramble to earn some sort of a living in order to raise her six children. Her an-swer was to turn her basement into a retail store. She had bikes, furniture, pianos — you name it. She'd buy up things in newspaper

THE THREE ROOKIES.
Left to right: My brother Fred, Uncle Bernie, Uncle Mel

ads or garage sales — anything she could sell for a profit. She also read tea leaves and told people's fortunes. In those days, the '40s and '50s, it wasn't uncommon for women to have a teacup reader at an afternoon tea party. A few ladies would get together and invite Maw to read their fortunes. She would study the tea leaves in the bottom of the cup after you finished your tea and tell your fortune based on her interpretation of the formation of the leaves. Maw was very good at it and was invited to all these teas and made money at it, with each person paying her 25 or 50 cents. Reading tea leaves and selling all these things from her basement — how on earth did she and her six children ever survive on that? When I got older I looked back and thought, This was one amazing woman. In today's society my grandmother Maw Rooke would be considered an entrepreneur.

I must have inherited my grandmother's business savvy and even her skill at reading tea leaves. When I was about 17, I went on a skiing weekend with a group of friends to St. Sauveur in the Laurentian Mountains in Quebec. We had a half day of skiing and then everything thawed and turned to slush. So we ended up in the hotel bar for three days, waiting for snow. For fun, and to kill some time, I said to my friends, "Okay, here's a pad and pencil. I want you to draw three trees, a road and a fence. Any way it comes to you." They'd each make their drawing, and then I'd analyze it and tell them what their drawings indicated, much like teacup reading. You can tell a lot from how people draw three trees, a road and a fence — about their family relationships, their careers, their hopes for the future — it's all there. I'd watch them as they drew. Did they take their time, were they slow and methodical, did they add little artistic touches on the trees, and so on? If so, they're creative and thoughtful. Or did they just whip off a drawing in 30 seconds? That means they're impatient, they want to get things done; they're not interested in details. So I'd observe things like that even before I looked at their drawing. And the picture itself would tell me lots of things. How do they see a tree? Is it large and shady or skimpy and bare-branched? The trees represent family. Are they all together, or are two trees together and one over there all by itself? That might signify a split in the family, a rift. Usually the person drawing the picture is the tree in the middle. The road represents your career. Where's the road going? If it's heading downward your career might be taking a dive at the moment. If it's going up, you're moving toward your goal. Is the fence blocking something? The fence represents your hopes and expectations. Is the fence alongside the road? If so, they're aligned.

The people in the bar loved my parlour trick and by the time the snow came, I'd read everyone in the room. One guy said he thought I must be a witch, because when I told him it looked like he'd turned a corner in his life — he had split with his family and moved to another city and started a new job — he stared at me and said, "How could you possibly know that? I did just separate from my wife, quit my job and have moved to another province." It was all there — I swear.

My Childhood and My Parents

My mother, Muriel Rooke (1915–2001), married my father, Frederick Fulcher, when she was just 17, pregnant with my brother, a situation not uncommon in those days. Then she had me when she was 19. She was still a teenager, with two young children. What kind of life did she have? I believe the only happy time she had was when she got out of the house to work on an assembly line in a munitions factory doing "war work" during World War II because all the men were overseas. She loved it. She made some great friends and a whole new life opened up for her. She couldn't stay home after that. She wanted to be out in the world, and who could blame her? Freddy and I were getting older and she wasn't needed at home so much, so she

Mom and Dad in 1940

got a job cleaning at a downtown hotel. Ironically, my mother never liked housekeeping, though our house was always spotless. But now she was getting paid! To have one's own money was very liberating, especially for a woman in those days. It gave her some independence, but it couldn't have been easy. The hours were long and it took two streetcar transfers and a bus ride to get to work. But I never remember her coming home grouchy or moody.

She wasn't a great cook, but we never went hungry. It was good, basic food. She had her routine. I'd know it was Monday because on

THEY DONATED TO THE BOMB VICTIMS FUND
These three little girls, Joan Padbury, Eleanor Fulcher and Barbara Thompson, held a bazaar at which they raised a sum of money for the Red Cross British Bomb Victims Fund.

We did our part for the war effort by holding a bazaar and donating the proceeds to the British Bomb Victims Fund.

Mondays we had meatloaf. Tuesday was liver and onions. Wednesday, pasta. Thursday, hamburger. Friday was fish and chips. Saturday was mashed potatoes and ground beef. Sunday was roast beef and roasted vegetables. That's what we ate every week and it was tasty and filling. We never had leftovers because there was never any food left over! When money was scarce, women didn't have the luxury of making too much food. You bought four pieces of liver and that was that. We ate a lot of white bread with our meals; it filled us up. Freddy could easily eat a loaf of bread himself each day. He was tall — 6 ft. 2 in. eventually — so it's no wonder. These days there are hundreds of books and millions of websites about proper nutrition — five servings of fruits and vegetables, the right balance of calcium, whole wheat, potassium, etc., but in those days we had no choice — we ate what didn't cost a lot of money. We survived and were healthy, energetic and happy.

I realize now we were a very poor family, but we didn't know it because everyone was in the same boat. We never had any money,

My favourite (and only) doll. 1943

Me, my dad, and Freddy

never owned anything. I found out later that we could have bought our house on Caroline Avenue for $2,000, but that was too much money back then. We had enough to eat, we had a lot of neighbourhood friends, we never locked our doors, we played on the street, everyone had a good time, and we looked out for each other.

It was the golden age of movies. There were dozens of wonderful, beautiful theatres throughout Toronto, like the Imperial or our local Joy Theatre at Queen and Jones. We could see a double feature for 10 cents. I loved movies, especially the musicals with Fred Astaire, Bing Crosby, and Gene Kelly.

Of course I loved my namesake, Eleanor Powell. My mother named me after her because she idolized her. That's why she enrolled me in tap dancing at age five — she wanted me to be a dancer and become a Hollywood star. That had been her dream.

I'm sure some of my lifelong "the show must go on" attitude came from my mother. My brother and I were expected to do our household chores without complaining or bickering. I saw her working hard, so she set a good example. Just as importantly, I knew my mother was proud of me even though she didn't praise me that often. I'd overhear telephone conversations when she'd boast to relatives or friends about my latest little accomplishment. She was always so encouraging about my dancing and brought everyone she knew to see me dance the lead in our many dance recitals. There was no way I was going to let her down. Her pride in me was a great motivator.

My childhood was full and happy. I had no complaints.

My Brother

My brother was named Frederick after our father and grandfather. Freddy (now Fred) lives in Winnipeg, Manitoba. Fred was always very bright and personable, and still is. He was 18 months older than me, so all through grade school I was the kid sister who came up after him. As a 12-year-old at Bruce Public School, he won the Athlete of the Year award for track and field, soccer and baseball. At his high school graduation at Riverdale Collegiate, he won the Dr. Steel Award for Leadership/Scholarship and Athletics. He was also president of the student council and earned a school crest for being on a city championship basketball team. Big shoes to fill! I couldn't wait to get to high school to get rid of the label "Fred Fulcher's kid sister." A bit of a pain, actually. At least when we were in different high schools I no longer had to hear, "Oh, you're Fred's sister." Yeah, yeah, yeah.

Freddy teased me without mercy. I used to hate it! One morning

Freddy and me in our house on Poucher Avenue, Toronto

at breakfast he pushed me too far. He said, *"I'm* going to have two pieces of toast and *you're* only going to have one!" That simple. But I had had it with the teasing. I wanted to hit him with something, anything, and what happened to be handy was a fork. Probably without even knowing what I was doing, I picked up the fork and threw it at him — and it landed right above his left eye and stuck there. If I'd wanted to hit him in that exact spot I could try a thousand times and never hit the target, but that's where it landed. If it had been one inch lower, I would have blinded him. Fred was stunned, sitting there with a fork sticking out of his forehead. I was stunned. My dad was there and he was stunned too, but not so much that he didn't grab me and throw me over his knee, and for the first time in my life, spank me. Dad finally removed the fork sticking out of Freddy's forehead and put a bandage over the wound. The next day, Freddy went to see the school nurse — no hospital, no doctor. He still has a little scar above his eye, and he and his family tease me

Freddy and me, 1943

all the time. "Oh don't mess with Eleanor — she might throw a fork or something."

I think about the bullying today in schools and on the Internet. I understand how when you're bullied you can get so mad that you just snap — and sometimes these kids have a knife or a gun. It's a very serious problem. I always tell my children and grandchildren to grow a thick skin and try to shrug it off and walk away. You never know who you're dealing with.

I had my first brush with violence when I was 15 or 16 at a local dance. I was with a girlfriend and whispered a few snide remarks about some butchy-looking girls across the room. One of them saw me do it, came over, grabbed the front of my coat and picked me up and slammed me against the wall. "Are you laughing at me?" she said in my face. Well, I've always been pretty good at thinking on my feet and I said, "What? No, no. Not you — those other girls that were in here…." She must have believed me because she let go. I snuck out the back way, afraid that she and her friends would be waiting outside for me. That was the first time I'd seen bullies picking on somebody, being physically violent — and I was the victim!

Freddy was a good hockey player and I thought at one point that he might play professionally, but after high school he took evening and weekend classes for seven years and got his Certified Public Accountant degree. (Mom and Dad couldn't afford to send him to university.) Freddy was very ambitious and went on to a very successful business career. He married his childhood sweetheart, Pat, and they have three children, Tim, Wes and Christy, and many grandchildren.

There were just the two of us growing up, which in those days was unusual — people had big families. Fred and I are extremely close; I love him dearly. I wish he and his family didn't live so far away so I

Fred, 1958

With Bruno, Fred and Pat, about 1977

My niece, Christy, is a talented singer. This is
the label of one of her CDs.

could see them more often. He is still musical but now focuses all
that ability in helping his beautiful and talented daughter, Christy,
who not only writes her own songs but sings professionally in her
own group and has released three CDs. Like father, like daughter.
Music seems to be in our genes. I am very close to Christy and always available for long chats about her personal life and her business
and singing careers. She's a very amazing young lady and I love her
deeply.

Young Talent and Tenacity

I was born May 22, 1934, in Toronto East General Hospital. The
house that my parents brought me home to was on Mortimer Avenue in the east end. When I was one year old, we moved to Poucher
Avenue. We lived there for three or four years, then moved to 11
Badgerow Avenue (around Gerrard and Carlaw) for the next five
years, then to 43 Caroline Avenue (around Queen and Pape) for ten

years. Around 1954, when I was 20 and out working, I moved to my own apartment — first in Scarborough and then to Northcliffe Boulevard (around Dufferin and Rogers), and finally to Clarendon Avenue before getting married.

As I mentioned, my mother named me Eleanor after Eleanor Powell, the actress and great tap dancer in the 1930s and '40s, so tap dancing was "my destiny," and by the time I was four or five years old I was taking lessons. When we moved to Caroline Avenue I was

Here I am about ten years old in a Beth Weyms annual recital. Professional seamstresses made the costumes and this one was for my Sailor's Hornpipe dance. I could do that routine even today!

about ten years old. I enrolled in the Beth Weyms dance school, a fairly large east end school. I walked back and forth to Beth Weyms for years, about a half-hour walk.

I got my first taste of show business during this time. Every year, I performed in recitals in front of an audience of 400 or 500 people at the Eaton Auditorium, which was on the seventh floor of the old Eaton's College Street store. And I *loved* it — being up on stage, the costumes, the stage sets, the choreography. I had discovered showbiz!

Dance school also gave me my first taste of teaching. In exchange for teaching the little kids, the four- and five-year-olds, I got free dance lessons. I found I really enjoyed teaching and was pretty good at it.

One year, three days before a dance recital, disaster struck while I was playing with some friends down on Eastern Avenue. In those days we made our own fun, and this particular day we decided we would hoist each other onto a roof with a rope and pulley — it was just one storey high, but high enough. But the kid who was pulling me up kept pulling and my hands were going around the pulley wheel. I kept yelling, "Stop!" but he didn't hear, and I had to let go. I fell to the ground and broke a bone in my left foot.

It was very painful but I didn't dare tell my parents because I thought my mother would kill me. They were not the kind of parents that would fuss over me and say, "Oh you poor little darling. Let's get you to the hospital." I was raised to grin and bear it. No sympathy, no doctors — we couldn't afford doctors anyway; there was certainly no OHIP. My mother would have asked me why I was doing something so stupid three days before a dance recital.

My foot ballooned up of course, and I had to take the laces out of my shoe during the rehearsal and the recital. I was responsible for my little four- and five-year-old charges — I was only ten or eleven —

and there I was, up in front on stage and leading them as though nothing was wrong; as though I wasn't in terrible pain from my foot, never limping, never showing anything was wrong. It was showtime, and you do what you have to do.

I got through the whole recital and never did go to the doctor, and as a result I had a lot of problems with that foot because the bone didn't heal properly. It would have been a simple thing for them to just set it and bind it up and make sure that it healed in alignment, but that was then and this is now. That foot's always been a little off. I can't wear certain shoes and still have some problems with it to this day.

I had the same kind of experience when my brother took me for a ride on his new bike, and my foot got caught in the spokes of the wheel. It broke the spokes and I twisted my leg really badly — I thought it must be broken it hurt so much. But what did I do? I apologized over and over to Freddy for breaking the spokes on his new bike. He was devastated. His new bike!

I remember a massive snowstorm in December 1944. Twenty-two inches of snow fell over a 24-hour period. Twenty-one people died, mostly from heart attacks, but one person was crushed when a Queen Street streetcar blew over on its side from gale-force winds! However, there was no question that I would stay home from school. "Off you go," my mother said, and I did. I could barely trudge through the deep snow up to my chest! But I did make it to school, only to find, of course, that it was closed, as was everything. I trudged home again.

I've always had that kind of "just do it" attitude. When I was 15, I got a summer job as a typist at Grand & Toy on Carlaw Avenue. The day before I was to start, I went to a corn roast on the beach of Lake Ontario with a bunch of friends, and we were wading in the water for a long time. It was early in the season and the water was freezing. It's cold in Lake Ontario at the best of times. Well, the next morning I woke up feeling very sick. I didn't know it at the time, but it was pneumonia. There was no way I was staying home though. So my first day on the job, I went to the office, feeling miserable. A woman was trying to teach me how to do something and I must have looked as lousy as I felt because she suddenly said, "Are you all right?"

I said, "No, actually, I don't think I am all right." I felt like I was going to pass out.

She said, "I think you should go home." So off I went. I could hardly walk. I remember trying to make it to a car where I could lean against it and rest for a minute, long enough to gather the strength to make it to the next car, and so on along the street. I was that sick that I didn't think I was going to make it home. But I kept going and did get home. My mom and dad's bedroom was right off the front hall, and I got in the door and fell onto their bed.

That was the only time my mother ever phoned for a doctor to come to the house for me. After he examined me that afternoon, I heard him talking to my mother. "She has pneumonia," he said. "She'll have to stay in bed for a number of days." And he gave her instructions about medicine and so on.

Then, I remember, my mother said, "Is she going to die?"

"No, she's not going to die, but she's very sick, so you're going to have to keep her in bed and make sure she takes the medicine."

"You're sure she's not going to die?"

This was becoming a somewhat distressing discussion. I could die?

Anyway, I didn't die. But I do have weak lungs because there's scar tissue that stays with you when you've had pneumonia. When I think back, it was pretty stupid of me to walk home when I was so sick I was ready to pass out, but that's how it was. You never thought of paying for a cab or asking someone for help. I knew that morning that I was sick, but so what? There was a job waiting for me. A job, a dance recital, a fashion show — you just go. Somehow you get through it. Yes, you might have died at the end of the day, but you just go and do it. It's called show business.

I'm not suggesting I was any tougher than any other kid in those days. That's just the way it was back then. Parents were parents, not "buddies." The world didn't revolve around the children's activities or self-esteem. Kids were not driven to school three blocks away. Kids today are often coddled. They're not being prepared for the real world. In sports and in schools, there are no losers. You don't fail. They often give trophies to everybody and you're allowed to try as many times as you need to get enough right answers or whatever. Well, real life is not like that.

My cousin Gay Fulcher

I loved to dance and took modern jazz and ballet as well as tap. I thought it was my calling. But then puberty struck. I discovered boys, and gave up my dance classes. I simply wasn't that dedicated. To be a dancer is all consuming and I could not see myself devoting that much time and effort. My talented American cousin Gay became a ballerina but gave it up when she got married. You have to love it. I loved it, and still do, as a way of expressing myself and letting go, but not to the extent that I was willing to give up everything else to become professional. To this day I have tremendous admiration for those who pursue it professionally, knowing the sacrifices they have made.

Planting the Seeds

Even as a child, I was really interested in clothes. I loved fashion. I used to be quite a little ham, posing for the camera. My Aunt Mabel was a clever seamstress and created her own designs. I knew she loved fashion, but what I didn't know was that she'd wanted to go to design school in New York but never could afford it. I was stunned in later years when my cousin Sharon showed me a scrapbook Aunt Mabel kept of me from the time I started my business — all the articles about me, everything. Maybe she was living her lost dreams vicariously. Anyway, that scrapbook turned out to be a blessing, as all my archives were destroyed. (More on this later.)

From the age of about ten to twelve, I used to make my own cardboard dolls. I'd draw them and cut them out and then make clothes for them. I'd design all kinds of outfits, colour them, cut them out and put tabs on each piece of clothing so it would stay on the doll. Then I'd build a little house for them on my bed with the sheets, with kitchen, living room, etc., and I'd play act — la da-dee da-dee da-dee, walking the dolls from room to room creating dia-

About 1942, posing for the camera

logue and dramatic situations. I was perfectly happy for hours in dreamland.

Soon I wanted my own clothes, not hand-me-downs — and it was up to me to buy them. When I was 13, I got a part-time job with Christie Brown Cookies — Saturdays from 8 a.m. to 3 p.m. I worked on the assembly line with a group of other teenage girls, and it was great fun. We'd sing and joke around and there was great camaraderie. There were eight girls, four on either side of a wide conveyor belt where row upon row of cookies came down the line. Our job was to pick up six cookies at a time and place them in a box until

Mom and me at Wasaga Beach, 1944. Every year my mom's sister, my Aunt Helen, rented a cottage. We were always welcome.

each box was full of 18 cookies. That belt moved pretty fast and we had to put them carefully in the box lickety-split, but sometimes they'd burst in your hands and fly up in the air. But they just kept on coming down that conveyor belt and you'd be scrambling to grab them before they passed you. It was just like that *I Love Lucy* routine where Lucy and Ethel are stuffing chocolates in their mouths and down their clothes just to keep up with the chocolates coming down the conveyor belt — could I ever relate to that scene!

My first paycheque from Christie Brown's was $3.73. I was so proud of having that job and earning my own money. I spent it immediately. A small store on the corner sold women's clothes, and every week I'd give the storeowner $2 against a $10 item and she'd mark it down in a booklet. Then when one item was paid in full I could start another tab for something else. If a sweater was $10 it took me five weeks to pay it off, but that was okay. I couldn't wait to get my own clothes. I wanted nice new things. The rest of my salary, $1.73, was for movies and fun money. I felt rich!

The Birthday Party

On the morning of my thirteenth birthday, which is a pretty significant time for a young girl, no one at home wished me Happy Birthday. So I was in a snit. I thought they'd all forgotten. The day went on, and after school I went to my dance class at Beth Weyms as usual, but instead of going straight home at 6 o'clock like I always did, I decided not to go home. I was mad — I'd been mad all day — so I fiddle-diddled around until 8 o'clock and then headed home. As I walked in the door, all my friends were leaving — they'd been waiting and waiting and waiting for me to show up for my surprise thirteenth birthday party! I nearly died. Since then, no surprise birthday parties for me ever again. If there's going to be a party thrown for me, I want to prepare, I want to anticipate — and I do not want to miss my own birthday party!

Miss Kennedy the Confidence Killer

I had a real prune of a teacher when I was in Grade 7. Miss Kennedy. I was a fairly good student and was always competing with another girl, Bernice, to be top of the class. I was also fairly extroverted. One day Miss Kennedy asked me to come to the front of the classroom and read something, and I got the giggles. I can't even remember what it was about, but something just struck me as hilarious, and I started laughing. Miss Kennedy was not amused. "Miss Fulcher, get control of yourself and sit down. Bernice, will you show Miss Fulcher how it's done?" Well of course Bernice got up and did it perfectly. Oh, she was a real creep, this teacher. She absolutely destroyed my confidence right then and there. I felt so humiliated. Looking back, I realize Miss Kennedy knew Bernice and I were competitors and asking Bernice to perform was a deliberate put-down to me.

From that moment on, I could not speak in front of an audience. I would not get up in front of people — I would shake, I was a wreck. You can't do what she did to me at that age. It's so harmful. Whatever confidence I'd had was shattered.

A teacher has a lot of power to influence a student for good or bad, and at that age — 12 or 13 — you're just developing your self-confidence so you're especially vulnerable. Even if you appear confident, you're not. You're trying, but mostly you're faking it. A good teacher has to be tactful when dealing with delicate egos. This incident stayed with me over the years and showed me how important it is to be sensitive to the feelings of others and never allow a situation to undermine a student.

The next year, I was lucky enough to get Mr. Whitley as a teacher. He was the opposite of Miss Kennedy. Mr. Whitley was tall and handsome and had a wonderful personality; just a wonderful man. He sensed something was wrong, because I'd always say, "No, I don't want to do that," when he called on me to speak. This very special teacher had a plan for me to start building my confidence. He started asking me, usually at the last minute so I had no time to worry about it, to get up and make a brief announcement to the assembly that such-and-such was postponed or something like that. Gradually I became more comfortable; every time was a little bit easier.

Years later, when I had my own business, Mr. Whitley came to see me about his two daughters, and we got to talking about my incident. He told me that Miss Kennedy would not take any boys in her class, that he had taken all her Grade 7 boys because for some reason she would not teach boys. She was a teacher who should never have been allowed to teach. Mr. Whitley remains my favourite teacher; he actually redirected my life. He knew that I was Fred's sister — Fred had been in his class the year before — and liked me, and saw that I needed to regain some self-esteem. Such a good teacher — I'll always remember him. Years later, I attended his funeral when I saw the obituary. I cried like our time together was yesterday. A good teacher stays with you forever.

My Hurry Bone: Track and Field

All my life I have been in a hurry, always wanting to be first, no matter what I'm doing. When I was a kid I was a fast runner. I represented my school at the Exhibition Track Meets, up to perhaps Grade 6.

Track and Field Team winners, Pape Avenue Public School. I'm seven years old—front row, second from the left.

Once, when I was in Grade 1 or 2 at Pape Public School, the principal called me out of my classroom. I didn't know what was going on. "We want you to come outside and race," he said. They were pitting me against this girl in the school to see who could win. It was strange. Just the two of us. I think I envied this girl. She came from a well-to-do family and had her own dollhouse, a dollhouse that was so big you could walk right into it! I wanted a dollhouse so badly I would dream about it. Anyway, some voice inside me said, This girl is not going to beat me. If the parents, who were present, think she can beat me, they're wrong. We took off from the starting pistol and I left her in my wake. That was the end of any running competition between the two of us. Can you imagine a similar situation today?

In those days, we were pretty stupid — we didn't know you should warm up before a race. We'd go outside and I'd hear that gun go Bang! and off I'd go. One day after I took off sprinting I suddenly got the worst pain in my chest and felt my heart contract. I stopped and collapsed — I just couldn't move — I thought I was having a heart attack. I just folded up and fell down. I was terrified. I never ran another race.

But I did eventually get my dollhouse — of sorts. One day my father came home to find me out in the backyard. I'd scrounged up four big pieces of wood, a hammer and some nails. "What are you doing?" he asked. I looked at him and said, as if it was a perfectly normal activity for a girl my age, "I'm building a dollhouse."

Pondo the Bully

The dollhouse wood came in very handy one day — as did my ability to run really really fast. Across the street lived a guy named Pondo, a big bully of a kid who used to pick on everybody. We were all afraid of him. One day I saw him beating up my brother in the lane behind our house — he had Freddy down and was punching him. I grabbed the nearest thing to use as a weapon, which was one of the boards that I'd been going to use for the dollhouse. What I didn't notice was that it had a long nail protruding at the end. Pondo was right on top of my brother so I went up behind him and whacked him hard on his backside with the board. The nail must have gone into his rear end because he went flying up in the air, leaping off my brother and taking off after me. I ran like the wind. I took off down the lane and around the corner and ran into our house and locked the door. Freddy was already inside by that time too; he came in the back door. As Pondo was chasing me, I remember thinking, I'm dead. If he catches me, I'm dead. But — he never bullied us again. Bullies pick on people who aren't prepared to fight for themselves. If you stand up to them they know you're not a pushover. I sent Pondo a clear message: if you ever come after me or my brother again, I'll pick up a board, a hammer, anything — to defend ourselves.

On the other hand, we kept our distance.

Pal and Other Pets

Pal was my one and only dog when I was growing up, a black-and-white miniature collie. He was like a person to me, my greatest buddy.

I was about eight; World War II was raging. Everyone was on rations. We'd get coupons to exchange for sugar or butter or whatever. My mother was out at war work and wasn't home when I got home from school — but Pal was always there. He'd jump all over me and we'd go out and play. Everybody in the neighbourhood knew and loved him.

One day we were all out playing ball on the street, and Pal was

Pal and me, 1941

Fuma, our loveable feline companion for 19 years

chasing the ball. A milk wagon came down the street and ran over him. Killed him.

I was in misery. All the kids were in misery. We didn't know what to do. We phoned the city and asked, "Where do you bury dogs?" thinking there was a dog cemetery.

"Oh," said someone on the other end, "we'll send somebody over to get the dog. We'll look after it for you." We all stood around Pal, waiting for someone to come. You know what they sent? A garbage truck. This man got out and picked up Pal by his hind legs, and threw him into the garbage truck. In front of all us kids. Every one of us was crying. We couldn't believe it. I never got over how they treated an animal in those days. He was my life, but to the city of Toronto he was just a piece of garbage. I never recovered from that incident and never got another dog.

We did have a cat that I loved, Mickey the bob-tailed cat. He didn't have a tail. We had Mickey for the longest time.

Many years later, Bruno and I found ourselves the owner of Fuma. We didn't really want a cat — we were just supposed to be cat-sitting for a few days as a favour to Angela. We both said, "Well, it's okay. It's just temporary." Nineteen years later we still had Fuma and we both had grown very attached to her. I'd hear Bruno come in after work and talk to her: "Hi Fuma, how are you? What did you do all day?" In November 2011, when it became obvious that she was nearing the end of her life — she had a big boil over her eye that our friend and veterinarian Chris O'Toole had drained twice — I said to Bruno, "Chris recommends we put her down. Her kidneys are weak, she can't see, and she can't digest her food."

"I'm glad it's you who's going to do it and not me."

I said, "You're really fond of that cat, aren't you?"

"Well, sort of, I guess." It was painless for Fuma because Chris put her out first. But me — not so much. Five days later I was still expecting to see her behind the big plant where she used to like to hide. Or waiting for me, like she did every day, when I came out of the bathroom in the morning. It hits you at funny times. Nineteen years — she was family. I didn't know I was that attached to dear Fuma.

Shorthand Studies

As I think back on those formative years, I remember another teacher who had an impact on my life, Mr. Waugh. In those days, as I mentioned, girls had four typical choices of a job: secretary, stewardess, teacher or nurse. So I was going to be a secretary. Which meant I had to learn shorthand. Which led me to the first day of Mr. Waugh's shorthand class — the day of my second great humiliation.

For some reason, I got a serious case of the giggles (again) when Mr. Waugh, a huge man, wrote PBTDCHAYJ on the blackboard. I thought it was the funniest thing I'd ever seen — I thought I was back in grade school scribbling on the blackboard. Well, Mr. Waugh turned around very sedately and said, "Do you find that amusing, Miss Fulcher?"

"Um, yes — a little."

He said, "Well, maybe you'll find this a bit more amusing. You go outside in the hall and you stay there for the rest of the class. We'll see if you find it so amusing the next time."

I was totally humiliated. He had pressed the right button with me — I had never been asked to leave the class. I stood out in the hall and got very mad. I'll show him, I thought. I'll show him that shorthand is a piece of cake. It turned out to be exactly that. Shorthand came very easily to me and I really excelled at it.

One day Mr. Waugh said to me, "Eleanor, would you like to come in at 3 o'clock when school's over? I'll dictate to you." I'd go in at

Grade 11 Student Council. I'm on the far left.

My Grade 11 class. I'm in the second row, second from the right.

3 o'clock and he'd dictate to me, much faster than he did to the rest of the students during regular class time. I got even better and faster. I knew I was being singled out but I didn't know why. I thought he was just helping me, which he was, but I think too that he was grooming me for the commercial school competitions they had for Grade 12 students who excelled at shorthand and typing. In any case, by the end of Grade 11, I was at the Grade 12 shorthand level.

Naturally, therefore, I was ready to quit school and get a job. I wanted to make some money. I wanted to buy nice clothes and makeup and look glamorous, and I didn't have any money apart from the $3.73 that I was making at Christie Brown's. When I told Mr. Waugh my intentions, he told me they were hoping I'd run for president of the student council the next year (I was on the student council in Grade 11), but if I was determined to leave, they'd help me find a job.

They made good on their word. The vice president of Eastern Commerce, Mr. Elliott, got me into Lever Brothers, a big company in downtown Toronto. It was a tradition of sorts that the top Grade 12 secretarial graduates of Eastern Commerce were hired by Lever Brothers. They'd be placed in the steno pool for three months and then be assigned permanently if they worked out. Apparently Mr. Elliott convinced Lever Brothers I would work out just fine, even though I was the youngest girl they'd ever hired. Thank you Mr. Elliott and Mr. Waugh for your great support.

As an aside, when I was writing this book I called Eastern Commerce to confirm a few facts and was amazed that the lady who answered had been there since 1968! We chatted and she told me she had taken one of my modelling courses — and her daughter had too. Her daughter now holds a senior management position with a large company and has to make many presentations on stage and in boardrooms. She told her mother that she credits the training she received at Eleanor Fulcher with enabling her to do this well. I was delighted to hear that.

CHAPTER 2

OUT IN THE WORKING WORLD

Lever Brothers

Lever Brothers was at the corner of Eastern Avenue and Broadview, not far from my house on Caroline Avenue, so I could walk there easily. It was a huge international company. There were six stories of offices plus a manufacturing plant.

All new secretaries started in the steno pool. I was there for a month or two, assigned to different men when their regular secretaries were off sick or on vacation. We typed the men's correspondence then showed it to the manager of the steno pool. If there was a comma out of place you had to retype the whole thing. No such thing as White Out to cover up your mistakes — and of course we used manual typewriters and carbon paper.

One day I was told I was going to work for Bruce Johnston, a Brand Manager, on the executive floor for two weeks while his secretary was on vacation. I'd never been up to the executive floor and I was very impressed and somewhat intimidated. I found out Bruce was being eyed for the presidency. Of the six or eight Brand Managers at the time, he was the brightest star. He had attended McGill University, spoke fluent French, had worked at UniLever in England (Lever Brothers' parent company), and he just happened to be a great-looking guy in addition to being creative, articulate, sharp and funny. Once, he shook up the rather staid executive floor by bursting through the doors wearing a cowboy hat and sporting fake guns (part of a promotion for a Lipton product). "This is a hold-up," he yelled. "Hands up!"

Bruce was an unorthodox worker. None of this 9 to 5 stuff for him. He liked to come in around 10:30 a.m. and work until 6 or 7, which was fine with me. Everyone else would leave at 5 o'clock and I'd still be there typing the letters Bruce wanted done that day. We got along very well, and towards the end of the two weeks, Bruce told the president he wanted me as his permanent secretary — to stay on even when his regular girl returned. The president told him that was impossible, that I was only 16 and barely out of school. I mean, there I was, a kid wearing bobby socks. I still didn't have enough money for decent business clothes. But Bruce made it happen. The president agreed to a temporary arrangement of three months. I nearly died I was so excited. I'm 16 and I'm on the executive floor, working for Bruce Johnston. After my three months were up, I was kept on as his permanent secretary.

Bruce changed the course of my life. One day he said, "Eleanor, now that you're going to be staying on the executive floor, perhaps you could take a few classes or something — something that will help you look a little bit older." I understood a little later that he wasn't just saying that I should look a little older — he meant that I should try to look a little more sophisticated and polished. I was starting to make some money so I'd be able to buy nicer clothes, and this sounded like a good idea. I investigated what kind of course I could take and found that there was a self-improvement course at the Walter Thornton Modelling School at Avenue Road and Bloor Street. I went for an interview and enrolled. When that course ended I continued with the modelling course because I was really enjoying it. I didn't think of myself as the model type, whatever that was. Little did I know that this was the beginning of the greatest adventure of my life!

The modelling course involved a lot of classes in walking and turning smoothly and gracefully. Because of my background and training in dance and body work, I knew right away that this was my field. The instructor was okay teaching the basics, but beyond that she didn't have the credentials of a former dancer. So I started mentioning a few things. For instance, I showed her an exercise in body alignment where you stand with your back against a wall, keeping the hips contracted, chest lifted, shoulders down, the small of the back touching the wall, legs taut and touching.

The teacher said, "Eleanor, do you have a background in this?" I told her about my training in ballet, jazz and tap, and she surprised me by saying, "Would you mind taking those girls over there and teaching them this move?" I agreed, of course — it was right up my alley, and that was the beginning of my teaching career in the modelling field. What a great fit. Thanks Mom!

Meanwhile, back at the office, I was starting to wear high heels and business-appropriate clothes — most of my money was going into my wardrobe — and I began to look more polished. In other words, I started to fit in.

Bruce was very happy with me and I with him. We really clicked, including our sense of humour. He liked that I never watched the clock. I didn't mind — I would have worked until midnight to help him finish whatever he had to do. I adored and respected him.

But then along came this woman, M.F., the head of Harriet Hubbard Ayer, a cosmetic line that Lever Brothers owned at the time. I think she'd been a professional singer from a wealthy family. She was tall and gorgeous. She was the only female in management. (Of course, they couldn't have a man in charge of a cosmetic line.) She had been given carte blanche to decorate her office and it was magnificent, with beautiful white broadloom and the latest in furnishings. I remember thinking, Would I ever love an office like that.

I read a line recently: Imagination is more important than knowledge. A very interesting statement. Well, when I saw that office of hers, I used to imagine having one just like it. What I was imagining, of course, was not only having an office like that, but being as powerful as this woman who was in charge of Harriet Hubbard Ayer. There weren't many women in those days that achieved that kind of status. But here was one, and I wanted to be like her. She had what I wanted.

Including, as it turned out, Bruce Johnston.

Next thing I know, this woman was engaged to my boss. She would come into his office while he was dictating to me and whisper all sorts of suggestive things to him, right in front of me. But if I tried to excuse myself and leave, he'd tell me to stay.

Lever Brothers was like a city — it was huge, and a lot of single guys worked there. There was a lot of dating among co-workers. Some of the men would come by my desk pretending to stop for something work related but they were really just checking me out. Bruce would witness this and ask me, "Wasn't that so-and-so from the fourth floor? What did he want? You're not going out with him, are you?" He was like a father, trying to guide me. "Don't date him whatever you do. He's got a bad reputation."

Along with the self-improvement course, Bruce knew I needed

some higher education. For instance, he was always trying to teach me words. He would dictate a letter to me, which I'd type up, and if I was in doubt about a word, I'd show it to Joyce, the secretary next to me, for her thoughts. Joyce would read the letter and say, "Eleanor, Bruce isn't going to use that word." He would use all these words that I could understand phonetically and get down in shorthand, but I didn't know what they meant. So I would look them up in the dictionary. She knew (and I knew eventually) that Bruce was only using that word so I'd be forced to expand my vocabulary. And it worked. To this day I am curious about words and am addicted to *The Globe and Mail* daily crossword puzzle.

Frankly, I don't think Bruce knew what to do with me. He saw something in me that I didn't know I had. It was like he was designing me, shaping me, like Henry Higgins in *My Fair Lady*. He taught me so much. He gave me a university education in the two years I worked with him.

I was in awe of him, of his brilliance. He was the greatest influence of my life. I owe him everything. My entire career could probably not have been possible were it not for him. But before long, I knew it was time for me to move on. It was now or never. I was getting too comfortable.

The Company of Women

At Lever Brothers, I worked with the greatest bunch of women. They were secretaries to all these young men who went out for their three-hour martini lunches and came back feeling no pain at 3 o'clock or 4 o'clock in the afternoon because they knew their secretaries could handle everything. Without a doubt, the company would have fallen apart without these bright, talented women. Some of them had been there for 20, 30 years. I was just a kid, but

I knew what was going on. The men got promoted and well paid, and the women stayed secretaries. It makes me sad even today to think of all those terrific women who just never had a chance. They probably would go to their graves never being recognized for how brilliant they were. They were so kind to me, showing me how things worked, helping me find my way around, showing me how to fit in.

My colleagues were intrigued by the modelling and self-improvement courses I was taking at Walter Thornton, and they wanted to know all about what I was learning. "Can you teach us, Eleanor?" So I started teaching. About eight of them were really interested, so during our lunch hour I'd take them into what was quite a large filing room and teach them what I'd learned. They loved it, and I loved it. I *loved* the teaching. They had helped me so much, I was happy to be able to give back something. I would show them things like how to walk from your hips, where you swing the hip around and the hip pulls the leg around and shapes the walk in and out. It was a walk we'd do so that you'd glide down the runway. It was a great look, very slinky and sexy.

Interestingly, several years later, one of these ladies called me. "Eleanor, I have MS, and I'm having trouble walking. I think that walk you used to teach us might help me." So I gave her about three sessions and she had it. She was able to walk without stumbling or limping.

After I'd launched The Eleanor Fulcher School of Modelling, long after I left Lever Brothers, these same women invited me back as a guest speaker at their annual dinner. I was honoured. They were still very interested and wanted to know all about my career. Such a great group of women. I am forever grateful to each and every one of them.

Changing the Course of My Life

One day I had an epiphany. I was about to enter the executive floor at Lever Brothers when I paused and glanced through the window of the door and saw all the secretaries typing away at their desks. And I froze. I thought, Oh my God. That's me in ten years. That's me — I'm going to be sitting there at one of those desks in ten years.

That was a crucial, pivotal moment in my life. It's the moment you realize you know what you don't want out of life. You may not know what you do want, but you most definitely know what you don't want. And I did not want to be sitting there 10, 20, 30 years from now typing in the open area while the men sat around in their offices. So I decided I was leaving. When I look back, sometimes I can't believe I did that, because I loved my job and I sure needed the money. But I knew I was now a very good secretary. I had a safety net because good secretaries were always in demand. It was *because* I loved my job, my boss, the women I worked with — that's why I had to leave. I thought, If I don't run now, I'll never, ever leave.

That was the day I handed in my notice. I told Bruce I was quitting because I was going into modelling. "Oh Eleanor," he said, "modelling is for tarts." Such was the image of modelling in those days. Naturally, Bruce was upset and concerned. But I know in his heart he understood. He wished me well and we remained friends.

By the way, Bruce eventually married a top model from Montreal. Hallelujah!

I've had a couple of epiphanies like that in my life (more on this later). It's like someone is tapping you on the shoulder and you can either ignore it and go on thinking, "Yeah, I know, but this is a great job and I'm earning good money and I have a great boss…" or you can say, "I can always fall back on this work; I can always be a secretary. But there's something else out there beckoning me. Something else is out there."

Learn to listen to your inner voice.

Modelling and Secretarial — A Foot in Both Worlds

I did fall back on secretarial work for that first year after leaving Lever Brothers because I needed to make more money than what I was earning modelling in fashion shows and teaching part-time at Walter Thornton's. Through the model agency, I was booked for a season to do some wholesale modelling at Poslin's on Spadina Avenue. They had a huge clothing line and a lot of clients, so they'd hire four models for the season. I sat in the back of the showroom where the clothes were hung, bored out of my tree between client showings, and said to myself, "I can't do this." I went to them after about the first week and said, "If you need any work done in the office, I have secretarial training." And the next thing I knew, they hired me permanently — they could use me as a model as well as a secretary in the office. The other three models finished the season and I was hired full time. However, I didn't like wholesale modelling so after a while I left.

I got a job at General Motors Acceptance Corporation (GMAC) and worked there full time for about six months while teaching modelling part time at Walter Thornton. It was awful. I knew it would be short lived, but I had to take it to build up some financial resources and then go back into modelling full time. I still didn't know what I wanted to do with the rest of my life — I was 18 — and I knew I didn't want to be a secretary forever, but I could do it for a short time when I was short of funds.

However, I quickly realized how exceptional Bruce Johnston was. My boss at GMAC was the complete opposite. Oh dear, my expectations were so high. But I did have an interesting experience at GMAC.

I had become very good friends with a co-worker who I'll just call "R." She was ten years my senior, single and very intelligent. She educated me, like Bruce had done. For instance, on our lunch hours she'd take me to different art galleries. I'd never been to an art gallery before. It was wonderful. At this time I was dating a man named Bill who was older than me by six or seven years. One night after work, R joined Bill and me for a drink. They got into an argument about me and R said to Bill, "You don't know how lucky you are. You don't deserve Eleanor!" Bill didn't even respond. He just kind of smirked.

Later, I said to him, "Well, what did you think of R?"

All he said was, "Hmm, very nice, hmmm, yeah, uh, huh." What did *that* mean?

Then one day R and I were out for lunch, and she said, "I love you."

"Thanks, R, I love you too," I said.

She said, "No Eleanor, you don't understand. I love you. I'm in love with you."

And I thought, Huh? It didn't make any sense to me; I'd never heard of lesbians. I told her so. She said, "How old are you Eleanor?"

I said, "18," and she laughed. "Oh, no wonder!"

I was so naïve!

Well, it became a little awkward after that because I had to see her every day. So I quit. I was ready to leave anyway.

I went back to modelling part time and teaching part time, and then once again ran out of money, so I took a job at Hayhurst Advertising.

At Hayhurst, at King and Yonge, I was doing secretarial work again, plus typing up advertising copy for the copywriters. One day one of the many young male hotshots who worked there asked me to type some copy. I took one look at it and said to him, "You want me to type up this copy? You think this is believable? Please." I can't remember the exact wording, but it was insulting to women. So I made some suggestions.

Though I didn't stay at that job for too long, I got valuable exposure once again to the advertising world and discovered that I loved it. It was creative, imaginative and exciting. I got a chance to do some copywriting, and there were some interesting employees. But it was not what I wanted full time.

A Seven-Year Contract, 1953–1960

I had been teaching part time at the Walter Thornton agency as well as modelling and working as a secretary just to make ends meet. I was still only 19 and trying to figure out where I belonged, trying to find myself. Along the way I was gaining great experience that would prove invaluable in my business.

A bit of background about the agency: Walter Thornton was owned by Gary Carter, who'd once been a business associate of Jack Kent Cooke — both very successful businessmen. However, they'd had a falling out and had gone their separate ways. (More about Jack Kent Cooke later.) Walter Thornton was the name of a top makeup artist in New York, and Gary Carter bought the name and opened up the Walter Thornton agency in Toronto. It was the only one of its kind at the time, and he was smart enough to see the potential. He also liked to be surrounded by models! It always seemed like more of a glamorous, fun business to him, like a Playboy Club — very popular at the time, lots of beautiful women — rather than a serious business.

Gary's wife, Dorothy May, was in charge of the school. (No one

Fur was the luxury fashion. I'm in the middle, in mink. We were in the Toronto Easter parade, about 1954.

knew they were married.) One day Dorothy May said to me, "I'm going to be retiring as director of Walter Thornton so I'll be interviewing five girls, one of whom will take over from me as Thornton's Associate Director, and I'd like you to be one of the five up for consideration."

The other four girls had many more years experience not only in modelling but also in teaching, and they were all older than me. At the interview session, Miss May, as she was known, handed all of us a form and asked us to complete it there and then. Since I'd been a secretary for three years, I was very accustomed to forms and filled it out quickly and handed it back to her. Then I looked around and saw that the other girls were still working on theirs. Hmmm, I thought, maybe I missed something — maybe there was another page?

I went up and asked Miss May, "Is there something on the back? Did I miss something?" No, no, I'd done it right. So I waited and waited and wondered what on earth these other girls were doing that was taking them so long. After she asked us all a few questions she thanked everyone, then asked me to come in to see her and Gary Carter. "I want Eleanor to be the new Associate Director," she said.

Gary Carter said, "She can't possibly run this place. She's only 19."

But Miss May told him she had faith in me and that I could do it. "Let's try it for two weeks, Eleanor," she said. "I'm going on vacation, and when I come back we'll see how you're getting along. In the meantime, we'll get your contract signed." My mother had to come in and co-sign the contract because I was only 19.

Miss May went away on vacation, and I was in charge. Oh God, I thought. Here I am, a teenager, with no experience, never having had an employee, and I was the boss of the entire staff! I could feel the animosity. They resented that I'd been brought in over those much more experienced. I could just imagine them thinking, What can she possibly know? I was in trouble.

Fortunately, I found a very popular book called *How to Win Friends and Influence People* by Dale Carnegie. I bought a copy and hunkered down. It said that if you want to get people to do something, you have to make it appear as though it's their idea. Give them credit for it and they're yours. Okay, I thought, let's start with that.

I already had ideas on how to improve the place. At Lever Brothers, I had learned — more than I had realized — good business procedures. First of all, I wanted to change the front desk. It was a mess, and the girl who sat there was wasting time drawing up forms manually. It would be much more efficient if she drew an original and ran off several copies. But I had to tread carefully because she was one of the gals who resented me.

"Lois," I said one day, "I don't know much about your job, but I see you working so diligently ruling and measuring these forms and I just wonder if there's not a better way of doing this. Surely we can help you out some way." I gave her a form I'd drawn up. "I'd love your opinion on this, so would you mind taking it home and telling me what you think we could do to improve it? Maybe it's something you can use; maybe not. But it might allow you to spend some time doing other things you're so good at, like talking to the students, because you're so good at public relations."

And it worked. She made some minor changes and that was that. We had them run off and her PR time improved 100 percent. And I let it be known that all the changes were her idea.

The teachers were the hardest ones because I was the new kid on the block. But I came up with a strategy to win them over too. I said, "When I was taking training here, I noticed that you were all really good at certain things. So I wonder if we could have each of you in charge of a certain area. We'll meet once a month and we'll hear any new ideas you might have for your area."

It worked like a charm. One was in charge of Runway, one was in charge of Makeup, one was in charge of Fashion, etc. It made a lot more sense than all of them trying to be experts in everything. We had a staff meeting once a month and I'd put on the agenda, "Lois is in charge of Reception and Booking, Leslie is in charge of all counsellors," and so on, and each staff member got ten minutes at the meeting to discuss their area and introduce any changes they felt were necessary. All I did was chair the meeting. I didn't tell them what to do. I made suggestions and let them find their own way. Thank you Dale Carnegie.

It didn't take long for them to start trusting me and we established an excellent working relationship. They came to me with any questions and we talked things out. I ended up getting along famously with the staff.

At the end of three months, Miss May told me the Associate Director job was mine permanently. I had to sign another contract — a seven-year contract. My salary was more or less what I'd made as a secretary and that never changed during the entire seven-year period. Gary Carter was not known for his generosity. The business was growing in leaps and bounds. Gary Carter would go away for six months at a time, then return and count his profits! He never once gave me credit for anything.

If a person was interested in taking a modelling or self-improvement course, she was interviewed by a counsellor, who then got paid a commission if the person signed up. I knew some of the counsellors were making more money than I was even though I was running the whole show. So I approached Mr. Carter and said, "If you won't give me any more money, then you'd better put me in sales, because they're making more than I am and I know I can do a good job."

He was all for it, because if I was that confident I'd probably bring in more money for him, but he said, "Well, can you do that and still be Associate Director?" I told him yes, I could do both.

It turned out I was a good counsellor. I always tried to be honest and empathetic. I really believed in the training and the students. I told the new students the realities of the field and what they could expect — either fashion modelling or commercial modelling. You had to be at least 5 ft. 6 in. for fashion modelling — now it's 5 ft. 10 in. — but for commercial modelling your figure wasn't as important as being suited to the part and having some acting ability. Then there was wholesale modelling, where you'd work on Spadina Avenue for the permanent wholesalers or at the hotels for the out-of-town manufacturers. Years later, when I was largely responsible for

They're building the kind of shape that makes a boss look twice. Teacher Eleanor Fulcher helps Mrs. Ursula Gutke of the Bank of Montreal slim those hips.

A *Toronto Telegram* newspaper article from about 1956 about a course Walter Thornton sold to companies to "polish" the office secretaries and receptionists. Here's an excerpt from the article: "Steps up the morale of the entire office to have some pretty girls around," says W.G. Munroe of Imperial Life. "We like our girls to round off any corners," says Robert Forsythe of Shell Oil.

"Some bad female traits — flat shoes, pony tails, too much makeup, gum chewing, rhinestone jewelry, sloppy clothes, poor posture — are not conducive to a mature attitude or sense of responsibility in business," says Miss Fulcher, a former fashion model who practises the glamour she preaches. In a series of five lectures, she teaches office girls such important tips as figure grooming and deportment, skin care and makeup, wardrobe sense and personal grooming tips. "Most of the girls enjoyed taking the course," says Miss Fulcher. "If a girl looks and feels her best she's satisfied with herself and works harder. Husbands and boyfriends take notice as well as their bosses, of course."

making sure Canadian models were hired before American models for the Eaton's and Simpson's fashion catalogues (more about this later), the models would earn photography rates of about $30 or $40 per hour, with steady work for weeks. That's where the big money was for high-fashion models.

By the end of the third year, I was advising Mr. Carter that he should really take the school concept across Canada. I'd become dedicated to the business and I knew it was ready to branch out. But he was too busy making big money in real estate and other investments. I could have really run with it if he'd wanted to go into partnership with me or offered me a business proposal. I would have stayed with Walter Thornton. But it's funny how things work out. Mr. Carter had no interest in spending money on expanding the business, so that opportunity never materialized. In retrospect, thank heavens it didn't.

When I started my own business, I thought I was starting from scratch, with nothing. But I underestimated the impact I'd had during those seven years at Walter Thornton. I had unknowingly built up my name by helping all those students that I'd spent hours talking to. I cared about them. I was just doing my job and loving it and trying my best to help them. All this effort paid off, because in later years those students were my best advertisements. People used to come up to me and say something like, "You know, my daughter went to you at Walter Thornton and you are the only one she remembers. When you started your own school she told everyone that's where they had to go."

At Walter Thornton, when the students got out of class, I would be on the stair landing so that I could greet them all and know their names. I had eyebrow pencils and tweezers tucked in my pockets. I chatted with them; I knew what classes they were taking. "You just finished Makeup? How's it going? Here, just let me touch up that

Demonstrating makeup technique at Thornton's

eyebrow. Let's look in the mirror.... How's that? Here, you do the other one now." (Recently, Oprah Winfrey had an eyebrow special-ist on her show. She was waxing here and there and fussing for the longest time, and I had to laugh. I could have done the same thing in thirty seconds!) Eyebrows were one of my specialties. Later, in my own school classes, it only took me two hours to give a lecture and demonstration and do makeovers on 25 students — half the face: base, powder, pluck brows, brow pencil, shadow, blush; they did the other half. I was fast — and they liked what I did.

I knew all the students by name. They got into the habit of asking me for a bit of help on this or that. I'd say, "Okay, you go to class. I'll

WALTER THORNTON MODELS
Place 1st... 2nd... and 3rd
in 1954 MISS TORONTO CONTEST

Left to Right: CATHY DIGGLES, "MISS TORONTO 1954"; JOAN HUNTER, 2nd; LOIS PITON, 3rd

CONGRATULATIONS
We Are Proud of Our Girls . . . and Our Teaching Staff

Cathy Diggles, left, was Miss Toronto in 1954 while I was teaching at Walter Thornton. She went on to be a finalist in the Miss Universe pageant. Shortly after, she married Gordon Richardson. Cathy and I have been lifelong friends.

As a finalist in the Miss Universe pageant, Cathy, right, caught the eye of Eddie Fisher.

talk to the teacher and we'll get you some extra help." Or they came to me and said, "Have you got a minute, Miss Fulcher? I've got a problem." I heard about situations with boyfriends, parents, school, you name it. I told them they would get through whatever it was. They trusted me. I loved being their teacher, counsellor, confidante and friend. I connected with my students. Being a teacher is very rewarding because you get constant feedback if you're any good. You feel that you're making a difference and you're being appreciated. I think a teacher is a teacher for life. And I had some great role models — Mr. Whitley, Mr. Waugh, Bruce Johnston.

In addition to dedicating myself 100 percent to my job, I gained loyalty from the staff. Within a year or two of my leaving in 1960, Walter Thornton closed their doors permanently. To replace me, Mr. Carter had brought in several business people, who knew nothing about the beauty field, to run the business. One by one his staff left. They phoned and asked if they could work for me. I told them I couldn't afford to pay them much and many of them said, "I'll work for nothing for two weeks, just to see if you can use me," and that's how my staff grew. So even though I hadn't been paid a salary worthy of my duties in seven years, it paid off in other ways. I can honestly say I've never worked just for the money. I had to love what I was doing, and that always paid off.

And that was the end of my Walter Thornton era, but I must tell this story: After my seven-year contract was up and I started my own business, Gary Carter sued me for breech of contract. I had nothing to worry about. I had put in my seven years and my contract was up, but he was trying to intimidate me like I'd seen him do with other models and staff so many times. I phoned him. "Mr. Carter, you can't intimidate me. I know all about intimidation because you trained me — I learned from a pro." He started to laugh, but he went ahead all the same.

Soon after I received notice that I was being sued by Cary Carter, I was at an engagement party for one of our models, Carolyn, who was marrying Jack Kent Cooke's son Ralph. Jack, a handsome and charming gentleman, was there, and I wandered over to him and we started chatting. I said, "I'm being sued by a former business associate of yours, Gary Carter" (his old nemesis). His face lit up. He wanted to know all the details, and I told him I wasn't concerned because the contract had expired. But this situation ran much deeper with Jack Kent Cooke.

"We'll get him, Eleanor." He told me to come by his office at 9 o'clock the next morning. I figured he may have had a few drinks and most likely would forget about it. I didn't think he really meant it. But at 9:07 the next morning the phone rang and it was Jack. "How come you're not here?"

I said, "Oh! Well, I wasn't sure if you were really serious."

"I'm always serious about business. Take a cab and get down here. I've got a lawyer with me." Oh my God. I went down to his office with my contract that clearly showed I'd fulfilled my obligation. Nonetheless, his lawyers got involved, and Gary Carter, after firing three lawyers, finally had to drop the lawsuit, which pleased Jack Kent Cooke enormously. An old, unsettled score between two business titans? Hallelujah!

Four years after I left Walter Thornton, Miss May died. I sent Mr. Carter a sympathy card out of respect. Miss May gave me my first big break at Walter Thornton. She had been the only one to see that I had some business smarts. That sympathy card led to him calling me and wanting to see me. It broke the ice between us. Since never once in seven years did he tell me I was doing a good job, I wanted him to acknowledge all I'd done for that business. My own business was now doing very well. I was at 667 Yonge Street; my husband, Bruno, had gutted the place and designed it and it was really very lovely. So I admit it — I wanted to rub it in a bit. I asked Gary to come at 5:45 because that was our busiest time, and I made sure he sat there for a few minutes and saw all these students, about 100 of them, checking in for their classes. I just wanted him to realize that it was me who had overseen the growth of Walter Thornton for seven years. We went out to dinner and all was forgiven. When I look back I can't believe how seriously I took that seven-year contract with no dollar amount in it. It would never hold up today.

A short while later I got the compliment (albeit indirectly) I had never received from Gary Carter when he called to make an appointment with me to meet his new ladylove. He asked if I would please spend some time with her — she could use some help with her makeup, etc. I said I'd be delighted. And so I did. He had finally acknowledged my worth.

A Need for Speed

As I mentioned, I have a hurry bone. I can't help it. I just need to go fast. That's why I was a good runner. I'm not sure I was such a great athlete or whether I was just always in a hurry to get to the finish line!

When I was 20, I decided I wanted a car. I saved up for driving lessons, got my driver's licence, saved my money, and finally had enough to buy a secondhand car — a Chevrolet. I was in such a hurry all the time that every time I got in that car I drove too fast. I loved it. Naturally, I got caught — too many times. I had lost all but three of my demerit points and they hauled me before a judge who said, "Well you know Miss Fulcher, you're going to lose your licence if you lose any more points." I thought, Wow, this is serious. I can't lose my licence! I honestly didn't think I could *not* speed once I was behind the wheel, so I took drastic measures and traded in my nice fast Chev for a secondhand Volkswagen. In those days, a Beetle could not do more than 40 miles per hour. Pedal to the metal — it didn't matter. That did the trick. I was forced to slow down.

I still have a little problem in the speed arena. One night, not that long ago, I was speeding, and a cop started following me. I pretended I didn't see him and just drove home. I pulled into the garage, then my heart sank as I saw that he had pulled into the driveway right behind me. I pretended to be rummaging around looking for something and going about my business — as if I would not notice a police car in my driveway! But the cop walked up to me as I got out of the car. I turned and got this shocked expression on my face and let out a piercing scream.

"It's all right, it's all right," he said.

"Officer, you almost gave me a heart attack."

"You didn't see me?"

"No. Why? What's the matter? What's happened?"

"It's all right. I didn't mean to scare you. But you were speeding back there. I'll let you off this time but you need to just slow it down."

If he had checked my driving history he'd have found out about my speeding demerit points and that would have been the end of my driving days. "Okay, thank you officer. I'm fine now. I'll be okay."

"Are you sure?"

That was close. Eleanor — slow down!

CHAPTER 3

The Eleanor Fulcher School of Beauty

The Big Decision

When I left Walter Thornton in 1960, I decided I would open my own school, The Eleanor Fulcher School of Beauty. It took a huge leap of faith that it would work — that I could make it work. At the same time, though, it was a natural progression, given my background. I loved the world of fashion and beauty. I knew I could run a business because I'd been doing it for years at Thornton's. I knew what a good teacher was. I had drive and ambition, I was a people person, I knew how to promote, and I hoped I had built up a good reputation.

I had been engaged (more on that later) to a wonderful man, but we had broken up. I truly couldn't imagine ever being in love with anyone else. That was my frame of mind at the time. I decided that I would date — go out and have fun — but my main focus would be my business. I also had a sense of adventure and a feeling that this was my time. I was 26, old enough to know what I was perhaps capable of achieving.

Above all, I had the passion.

Today it seems like people want to make money immediately. In my experience, you've got to love what you do, work hard, and the money follows. Money wasn't the prime motivating factor for starting my business. I just wanted to do what I loved doing and make enough money to pay my bills and have a little left over. I thought, I've got to try this. I can always be a secretary but this is something I've just got to do. I had no intention of competing with Walter Thornton. I decided I would specialize in self-improvement rather than modelling, and I'd cater to the over-25 market, a group of women Walter Thornton had sadly neglected. So I designed a program accordingly.

No Money — Big Idea

I knew I needed a great location for my school. It had to be in a good area, have some street presence, and be accessible by TTC — public transit. But I had no money saved for renting a place — so I came up with an idea. The Joseph Bobyk Hair Salon had recently opened at 186 Bloor Street West at Avenue Road, and it was perfect for my needs. Well, I thought, I may as well start at the top. I phoned Joseph Bobyk and arranged a meeting and pitched my idea.

"I'm starting a school of beauty," I said. "Now, I see you don't use your salon three nights a week — Monday, Wednesday and Friday — so if you agree, I'd like to use it for my school on those nights you're closed." I told him I would send all my students to him to do their hair for an agreed-upon rate, and they might turn into permanent clients. Also, I would stock his salon with the

My first ad

makeup line I was using — Irene Kent — and he'd get a percentage of the sales.

The greatest shock of my life was when Joseph looked at me, smiled, nodded and said, "Okay." He shook my hand — we never had a written agreement — and said, "When do you want to start?"

Great! I had the space, I had developed the program, and now I needed students to come and take my courses. And of course, first they needed to know the school existed!

My advertising background came into play for my first ad. I stood on the sidewalk at Avenue Road and Bloor and spotted a woman about 30 years old who had gorgeous bone structure but had very

Before and Afters became our specialty.

little else going for her. I walked up to her and said, "How would you like to have your hair cut and styled and your makeup done — a complete makeover? I can't pay you but we'll give you these services free of charge — and you'll receive a beautiful 8 x 10 glossy picture." We talked for a bit and she enthusiastically agreed. We did the "before" shot, then I did her makeup, Joseph Bobyk did her hair, I draped her with my white fox stole, and we did the "after" shot. The difference in her was astonishing. She was thrilled, and I had my first dramatic "before-and-after" photo.

Taking Care of Business — Early Days

I now had the before-and-after photo for an ad in the newspaper, but there was one small problem — an ad in the *Toronto Star* would cost about $500. I didn't have $500. I'd never been able to save any money because everything I earned went to rent and living expenses. I'd have to borrow the money from the bank. I made an appointment with the bank manager, who said, "What kind of business are you starting?"

I explained my business plan for the Eleanor Fulcher School of Beauty and concluded with, "I need $500 to place an ad."

"I don't think we can do that," he said. I had no credit rating because I'd paid cash for everything in my life. I never ran up debt. But apparently that made me a bad credit risk! Never mind that I had been the Associate Director of Walter Thornton for seven years. Not good enough. That's when my wonderful brother, Fred, my white knight, agreed to co-sign the loan. Problem solved. I paid back the $500 as promised, with the bank manager looking over my shoulder whenever I visited the branch to make a payment.

Later, when I needed to borrow $2000, I went back to that bank but they refused me again. So I shopped around. At the Royal

Bank, the manager said, "Hmm, school of beauty. My wife loves makeup — is that what you're going to do?" I explained the program in detail. "That sounds like a good idea. I like it." And he approved the loan. Finally, a male bank manager who understood the value of my business. A bank manager with vision!

When I look back, trying to get that initial bank loan was indicative of how really tough it was for a woman to borrow money in those days, never mind start a business! It was a great learning experience that I passed on to students by suggesting they borrow $500 from the bank to pay for the course and instead of paying us weekly, pay the money back to the bank. In doing so they'd start to establish their credit rating. These practical matters of personal finance weren't taught in school. Many took my advice and were happy when they had no trouble later in getting credit to buy a car or even a house.

So now that I had created an ad from that before-and-after photo, plus the $500 loan, I was ready for business. I placed the ad in the *Toronto Star* — and it worked. The phone started ringing!

I had asked Joseph if it would be okay for me to put in a phone line at the salon. I'd work from home but have the same phone line put in at his salon. He agreed. My first ad appeared in the *Toronto Star* on April 4, 1960. When people saw the ad and phoned the number, I'd answer, "Eleanor Fulcher School of Beauty," in my best telephone receptionist voice.

"Yes, I'd like more information please."

"Could you hold, please? I'll see if Miss Fulcher is available." I'd go away for a minute, come back, and put on my most professional voice and say, "This is Eleanor Fulcher. May I help you?"

I also okayed it with Joseph that I could put up a temporary sign in the front lobby on the nights I was using the salon. Every Monday, Wednesday and Friday, I'd arrive early carrying my little placard that said Eleanor Fulcher School of Beauty. I hung it on the door using a tiny nail so it wouldn't leave a permanent mark. "You'll see our sign in the foyer," I'd tell them over the phone. When I left at night, I'd take my sign home with me.

My strategy when I opened the business was to cater to women 25 and older, because it was a demographic that was being neglected in the beauty field. Walter Thornton didn't encourage anyone over 25. (Gary Carter told everyone they'd be called an old maid when they turned 25 if they weren't married.)

My first program was five weeks: Skin Care, Makeup and Hair Styling. The cost was $95. I interviewed all the women on Monday evening between 6 and 8 p.m. (I told them that was the only time slot available.) Eight women enrolled, all married, over 25. We met every Wednesday evening at the Joseph Bobyk Salon and I personally taught them skin care and makeup and Joseph did their hair. When they finished the program I said, "It's a shame the five weeks are up because I'd love to help you with posture, poise and fashion." Their response was, "Eleanor, our husbands are thrilled. Anything you want, we'll do it." All eight agreed to another five weeks and after that, all eight wanted the modelling training. So in spite of starting my school with the intention of a five-week program for the over-25s, I was unable to restrict myself. I wanted so badly for each of them to develop their maximum potential — and so did they.

Within a few months I opened the door to teens, young adults, seniors — come one, come all! I changed the name to Eleanor Fulcher Self-Improvement and Modelling School. It was quite incredible how it took off.

I called the program for "older" women — 25 and up — the Dynasty Programme, because *Dynasty*, the TV show that was popular at that time, was changing the image of women. Women over 25 had only been seen as housewives and moms, but suddenly advertisers had to rethink their over-25 concepts. These Dynasty women

We offered a wide variety of courses and programs

Modelling course brochure, 1981. A talented graphic artist named Brig created my logos and illustrations for a lot of our printed materials.

Teen Butterfly Connection

A brochure for our Makeup Artistry course

Dynasty Programme

"Diamonds are only a girl's second-best friend...

Meet Number One!"

Competition has never been keener than in the 80's both in the market place and in the dating race.

I'm Eleanor Fulcher and I can give you all the poise and confidence you need in today's competitive world.

Take one of my courses and learn the secrets crucial for success image — skin care, makeup, figure, wardrobe, hair style, walk, communication.

The woman of the 80's needs every advantage.

You've got me — isn't that what best friends are for?

ELEANOR FULCHER

self improvement • model school • model agency
personalized cosmetics • boutique • health spa
667 Yonge Street, Toronto, Canada M4Y 1Z9

Career Woman Update

THE ELEANOR FULCHER Career Woman Update

Left: Modelling & Television

Right: Image and Personality

MODELLING & TELEVISION

Modelling today enjoys a broader base than ever before. Different types of models - the cover girls on the fashion magazines, the housewife on the television commercials, the high fashion runway model - are constantly being discovered to work in this most glamorous of all professions.

Determination, enthusiasm and a true sense of personal and business image combine to maintain a standard of excellence that is without equal for everyone trained at THE ELEANOR FULCHER SCHOOL.

IMAGE & PERSONALITY

Before / After

Image is the secret of a person's confidence. This is truer today than ever before. As the pace of life increases, more emphasis is placed on appearance as a means of assessment. This is a reality no one can afford to ignore.

Fortunately, the myth that beauty is born, not made, has been dispelled and the wise person is taking advantage of modern methods to improve upon nature. These techniques, coupled with a positive personality, are the foundation of a person's confidence - and the foundation of ELEANOR FULCHER training.

ENQUIRE ABOUT THE ELEANOR FULCHER SPA VACATION ON BEAUTIFUL LAKE MUSKOKA

Beauty...

Personality

Modelling Techniques

Photography

Television

Practice Classes

Workshops

Lectures

Tone & Trim Classes

Three pages from a brochure

were dynamic. They had class, elegance and fashion chic. They looked anything but old — they looked sensational, sexy and worldly. It was always exciting to watch them strut their stuff.

We had lots of programs so we could steer everyone into the most appropriate area. For instance, I started an introductory teen program that helped build confidence. It was called The Butterfly Connection. I also had children's courses, Career Woman Update, adult self-improvement — eventually for men, too — modelling, image, personality, television, acting, and male/female group training. In 1980, Toronto was becoming known as Hollywood North because so many movies were being made here, and there was a huge demand for makeup artists. So I joined forces with George Abbott, one of the leading makeup artists in North America at the time. George designed our film, photography and stage makeup courses. The program was the first of its kind in Canada and covered all facets of the profession, from aging techniques, scars, bruises, blood, fantasy, monsters — all that and high-fashion makeup of course.

Staff 1961-1962 at 15 ½ Bloor St. West, Toronto, my first location

Makeup class

If people didn't want to sign up for a course, they could simply book a makeover or have their colours done (both makeup and clothes), or come to a one-day Image Update Seminar.

Preparing Models for the Runway, Camera and Life

I was totally upfront and honest about modelling. I told prospective students it was a good field but very competitive, and they shouldn't get their hopes up that they'd become top models. I'd assess them and tell them they probably wouldn't be able to do photography or this or that, maybe because of their body structure or a facial feature or something. I always emphasized that the purpose of the courses was to bring out their best features and help them find their individual style.

Mary Smith (not her real name) was one of my modelling students and ultimately became a teacher and model. She wasn't happy with the amount of modelling work she was getting. I was honest with her. "Mary, your look isn't 'in' right now unfortunately." She had an aquiline nose, very beautiful — and it's very in today — but in those days everyone wanted the same look — the cute little turned up snub nose. All the successful models had "the look" and if you didn't have it, it wasn't going to happen for you. Mary decided to have surgery on her nose and voila — she became one of the top photographic models. Though I understood why she had surgery, I was sad that she felt that pressure. But that's the way it was. She was prepared to do whatever it took. That's ambition. That's dedication. Years later, after retiring from a successful modelling career, she opened her own business focusing on her own line of makeup — very successfully, I'm happy to report.

It's different today. Top models can have many different looks. You can have a beautiful aquiline nose, strong features, a square face, oblong face, etc. The fashion and beauty industry now encompasses all cultures and types.

Cosmetic surgery wasn't talked about a lot in those days; it was very hush-hush, not like today when everyone's more open about having things done to their face and body. And the surgeons back then were not nearly as experienced in that type of cosmetic surgery, so it was somewhat risky. You'd think long and hard before putting yourself through that.

The key is to find a doctor who is passionate about his or her work. This I know from first-hand experience with my son, Marcus, when he was about seven years old. He had ripped his bottom lip open and we'd had it stitched at the hospital. Hardly a scar. Shortly after this, he fell off a monkey bar at the local park and split it open again — in exactly the same place. His lip was now mush. We rushed him down to Sick Kids hospital. All the while I was thinking, His mouth will be deformed. Marcus was such a beautiful boy, and I thought that he was going to be marred forever. How could that lip ever look the same again? At the hospital, the nurse took our information and said, "You're so lucky. Dr. 'T' is here today. He's over from England and has had to specialize in lip surgery for two years to get his residency papers. He's fantastic. He'll operate on your son, so don't worry." Oh thank you God, for sending us Dr. T that day. He operated on Marcus's lip and it was nothing short of a miracle. He had his lips back. You could barely see the stitches. Such beautiful work! Dr. T was truly an artist. If you are blessed to find a doctor like that, who is passionate about surgery, you are indeed lucky. There's no doubt in my mind that had Marcus been attended to by another doctor with less "lip" experience, he would have had a deformed mouth. Dr. T did nothing less than save my son's future life. So I most certainly believe in cosmetic surgery. But there are limits. When I look at some of the Hollywood stars that have tried to stay young looking instead of growing old gracefully, it's very sad. Their faces are unrecognizable, almost grotesque.

Marcus in 1976

I wanted to learn more about this doctor who had performed this miracle on my son. I invited him to my office and I found that he was exceptional at what he did because it was not just a job to him. It was his passion. And that's what makes the difference in life. Good is not good enough. When you want perfection in whatever you do — when it goes beyond doing something for the sake of just getting paid for it — that's when you become extraordinary in your field. So we met, and it turned out Dr. T and I had mutual interests and respect. After all, he was in the beauty field too. We became good business associates. At my invitation, he came to our school and lectured, showing before-surgery and after-surgery pictures. Amazing, life altering — as was our training. Surgery was a last resort if someone couldn't accept a particular flaw — as they saw it — in their features.

The school was all about giving students a strong foundation for whatever their future had in store. I wasn't just interested in successful models; I was interested in successful lives. I always sold the confidence factor. If you had the confidence of a model and you could look like a model, you could use that everywhere. I knew from experience that that was the key. You had to not just look the part, you had to feel the part and be the part. True, they would have to go out there and learn from their own mistakes, but they would be armed with powerful tools to deal with it. Today it seems that models can be plucked off a seat in McDonald's and wooed with money and glamour. But they don't have any training. They don't know what pitfalls might await them. And they don't realize that modelling is a steppingstone. It's not going to last forever. Some models are going to be good for ten years, and then what? Then they're yesterday's news. Suddenly their look isn't needed anymore. Our training prepared them for life beyond and apart from modelling, helping them use the knowledge they were gaining from modelling to prepare for the next stage in life, their next career. The aim was to guide them properly into rewarding and fulfilling lives. Whether or not they made it in modelling was secondary because one way or another they had to first feel good about themselves. Hundreds of our graduates went into very good post-modelling careers, such as Caryl Baker and Jean McDonald, who were two of my first graduates and eventually founded their own cosmetic companies. Judy Welch started her own successful modelling agency. Many went on to good marriages, too. Beauty will always attract — so from a dating point of view, there are many more choices available. For example, one of the winners of our Model of the Year award, Velvet Richardson — beautiful, outgoing, bright — married the man who was one of the

A Model of the Year, Velvet Richardson, and her husband, John Haney

Velvet and John Haney

original financial backers of Trivial Pursuit, the board game. I bumped into her and her husband recently at a fundraiser, and we hugged and chatted like it was yesterday. She still looks sensational. Some of our successful models are still as glamorous as ever — it never fades. Once a model, always a model.

My friend Andy Body, who was my choreographer for many years, tells me, "Eleanor, you have no idea the number of models out there who remember you fondly and want to know how you're doing." That makes me happy. I hope in some way I helped them to fulfill their dreams.

As for the modelling world today, everything happens too quickly. Headshots are emailed to Paris, there's overnight acceptance, and the models are on the next plane. I get very annoyed when I hear about 16- or 17-year-olds being sent to Europe, sometimes without chaperones. At that age they are not prepared for everything that's going to be thrown at them, and it's unacceptable that they should be exposed to all that without the proper grounding — call it advice, guidance, training, whatever. Maybe that's the mother in me talking, but I can't stand the idea of these kids having no idea how to react in certain situations. For instance, what if a client makes a pass at you? How do you deal with that? Do you slap him? Do you shake a playful finger at him and say, "Uh-uh, that's not in our agreement," and treat it lightly? Young women have to be prepared for all kinds of situations. These days, models become supermodels — celebrities — and often, they are not prepared for that kind of adulation. The same thing happens to young musicians and actors. Overnight sensations in an unreal world. It's too easy to start believing the hype and losing yourself. When I ran my business, I felt strongly that our models would have a good, solid foundation and be prepared to deal with whatever situation arose in our field.

Through Fulcher's Line Model & Talent Agency, a division of

Eleanor Fulcher Limited, models were hired for a variety of media. Here's what the booking line-up might look like on a typical day:

- In print: Jill Duggan for The Bay shoot
- Simone Butchers with Kellogg's All-Bran photo session
- Bryan Johnson with Olympia Tiles TV commercial
- Four models for the Village Shop and Festival of Fashion
- Television, six models on *Seeing Things*
- Film: Rebecca Nordstrom in a rock video
- Promotions: four models in Dimension Travel, Hitachi, Nissan and Cineplex Odeon.

Jill Duggan was a model in great demand

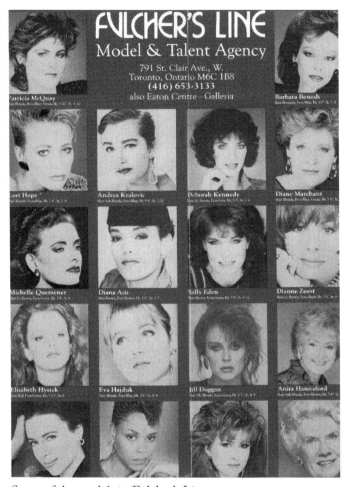

Some of the models in Fulcher's Line

In those days, there wasn't a lot of photography work. Promotions and events were a good source of income, though. For instance, Rothmans might ask for two models to hand out cigarettes at a cocktail party promotional event (not any more!). The type of model that was good for this kind of assignment was one who was personable and could handle a crowd and could handle a man who'd maybe had one too many drinks. I wouldn't send just any girl to something like that. I had maybe six or seven really good promotional models that had great personalities and could handle any man who was getting a little too friendly without being rude to him. They were perfect ladies. They could put him in his place with a smile and such aplomb that he never even knew he'd been put in his place. That was an art. Personality always played a part in being a good model. Personality, attitude, work ethic — the whole package.

Whatever field you go into, you need to talk to someone who's been there and done that, hear what they've learned, what's good and what's bad. Sometimes you have to be told that you might have to audition many times before you get a "yes." I remember Jill Duggan, one of our very successful models, telling me years later that she auditioned 26 times for TV commercials before a client said yes. Then, finally, all the doors swung open. It's called determination. And having self-worth. You won't be able to withstand 26 auditions if you don't have all that and more — you have to know in your heart what you want. It takes guts, determination and faith in yourself. If *you* don't believe in you, no one else will.

It's not easy to be successful. It doesn't come with a wave of a wand. If it did, it could disappear just as easily. You have to earn it, and the way you earn it is to be persistent and know what your goal is and just keep at it.

Models with big egos are not going to last. They can come and go in a month, because the clients don't want "attitude." Clients want someone who is committed, determined, open to ideas, willing to try something new, accommodating, easy to work with. You have to respect other people. If you're modelling a dress, for instance, you might disagree with what the photographer is doing, but you don't just say, "Well, that's wrong. I don't like that." If you have an idea, suggest it and ask if *both* of you could try it out — get his opinion.

In addition to running the school, I decided to offer a training program to corporations. It was received very enthusiastically. I trained

25 female employees at a time, concentrating on corporate image, poise, hair, makeup and fashion. My goal was to help women get ahead in the corporate world. The Group Training program was very successful in more ways than I had imagined. Most of the women in this five-week program would invest personally in more training at the school. They could see its value and were anxious to learn more.

My First Office, 1962

The early days of the Eleanor Fulcher Self-Improvement and Modelling School were hectic, busy and exciting. The school grew very quickly. My arrangement with Joseph Bobyk worked out beautifully. As lifelong friends, Joseph and I have often reminisced about those early days with great pleasure. Years later, Joseph confessed to me that my timing was perfect because he was in over his head financially when I'd come to see him. When my business took off his took off too, and he was able to climb out of debt and establish one of the top salons in Toronto. The Irene Kent line of makeup and skin care products were selling very well. We used these products in our makeup classes, and once a woman tries a brand of makeup and likes it, she sticks with it. My handshake agreement with Joseph ended only because Toronto was planning the Bloor subway and he had to move. Joseph got his own place on Avenue Road, an exquisite salon, and I moved on to my next location, another hair salon on Bloor Street West near Yonge. I had the same arrangement I had with Joseph. I couldn't believe my luck.

In addition to using the Bloor Street West hair salon on Monday, Wednesday and Friday, I rented for a pittance a small office at the back of the building. My first office! I was thrilled with it. Even though it was small, it was very important to me and I tried to make it as nice as possible. I actually had a permanent office. I was on my way.

The Bloor Street salon was owned by a man — we'll call him "K" — whose wife ran it. He said he was in the windows business. Now, if you were casting a movie and needed a meek, mild accountant, K would be perfect — a little guy with glasses and a kind face. One day he said, "Eleanor, I want you to take over the salon. We're going away for a while. My wife's health isn't good. She needs to get out of the business and take a vacation."

I said, "Well that's great, but I can't afford to buy this salon."

He said, "No, no, I don't want you to buy it. I'm giving it to you. You just take over the day-to-day expenses."

Now, his wife, J, and I got along famously. We'd shopped together a few times, and money was not an object to her. She would see a pair of shoes she liked and buy them in four different colours, bringing out a huge wad of cash to pay for them. Of course I noticed this and was very impressed. I thought that the salon must be doing really, really well, and all the customers must be paying in cash. How naïve!

I had met my future husband, Bruno Arnold, at that point, and one day we went for a drive west of the city and decided to pop in on K and J. She had told me where they lived and invited us to drop in if we were ever in the neighbourhood. We decided to take her up on her offer. We parked the car, went up to the front door, knocked, and J opened the door. She looked like she was going to have a heart attack. I just thought she was a little excited — a little too excited, since it was just Bruno and me standing at the door — but it was soon obvious she was in a bit of a panic. "Oh! Eleanor! Do me a favour. My husband's in a meeting right now — come around to the back." We went in the back door to the kitchen and J excused herself and went into another room. As she returned, I caught a glimpse of some men sitting around a large table. Still didn't think anything of it but I did think it was strange that she was such a wreck.

There was another incident. At one time J and I were talking on the phone when she said, "Eleanor, I think our phones are being tapped so let me call you back, okay?"

"Why would your phones be tapped?" I said.

"I don't know, but I just have this feeling."

Fast forward…One day the newspaper headlines read that K has been arrested for murder and is suspected of being a hit man. What? Our conservative-looking friend in the windows business? I thought back to the meeting we'd witnessed at their house, all those men sitting around the table. No wonder J was a wreck. If Bruno and I had been able to identify any of them we could have been in danger. I remember saying to J at the time, "Oh I can see K's busy — bad time. So we'll just get going." We have never just "dropped in" on anybody since!

K went to jail and J disappeared. But because we'd associated with them through the salon, Revenue Canada audited my books every year for five years. Later, when I hired a new accountant, he said, "Eleanor, why are you being audited every year?"

I said, "Isn't everybody?" He paid a visit to Revenue Canada to enquire why they were picking on a woman trying to run a small business. They stopped auditing me. All those years, they must have been looking for a connection. So if something — like a wad of bills — sounds too good to be true, it probably is.

Relocating and Growing Fast

The business was taking off and we soon outgrew the Bloor Street West location. I knew I needed a central, permanent location that had some prestige. Plus, it had to be easily accessible by TTC. Enter my husband's area of expertise — architecture.

Bruno called me one day and said he was taking me to see a place on Yonge Street — 667 Yonge. Well, it was the worst space you've ever seen in your life. Dark, dingy, smelly — depressing. It had previously been used to house animals. My heart went out to the former tenants! I couldn't wait to get out of there. But Bruno — thank God he is who he is — said, "Do you like the location?"

"Oh," I said, "the location's fantastic! But you've got to be kidding. How could you possibly bring me here?"

"But do you like the location?" He kept pounding away about the location, location.

"Of course I like the location!"

"Well that's all that matters. Because we're going to gut it anyway."

"Oh, we are?"

"That's right. You're going to show me what you need and I'll completely redesign it."

We went to a restaurant and I drew on a napkin what I wanted. "Well, you'd have to come up the stairs and go into the reception area, which should be here. And then the counsellors' offices should be next to Reception, here. Down the hall there'd have to be a large room for training…." I'm sketching all this on a napkin. That's all he needed to draw up the plans! We signed the lease and got the space. That was the most interesting lesson I ever learned, because never in a million years would I have moved to 667 Yonge Street if Bruno hadn't persuaded me.

When he finished renovating, it was perfect. There was even an extra little room near the back exit. Bruno suggested we rent it out. I said, "What kind of company would rent that dinky little hidden room at the back?"

A security company, that's who. It was exactly what they wanted: a small space, kind of hidden away, with no sign, just big enough for one person to take calls if there was a security problem with one of their clients. The fact that it was in the back of our building was a big plus because the employee didn't even have to come in and out the

Late 1960s in front of my school at 667 Yonge Street, Toronto. My sisters-in-law (Bruno's brothers' wives) and my niece visited us from Switzerland. *Left to right:* Monica Arnold, Rita Arnold, me, and Katrina Arnold, our niece.

My sister-in-law Monica Arnold is a wonderful artist. This is one of her original paintings.

front door since there was a door in the back. We never saw them — and they paid almost one-third of our rent! Bruno, you're a genius.

What was also great about 667 Yonge was that downstairs was Landau's, a ladies' clothing shop. I got to know the owner and she got to know my taste. She would select clothes from her new shipments and put them away before anyone even saw them. She knew I had to look good and I needed a wardrobe suitable for TV, lectures, etc., preferably one-of-a-kind — without a huge price tag. She picked out fabulous clothes for me in all my best colours. She knew I didn't have time to shop so she became my personal dresser. What a great arrangement that was.

Soon we needed even more space. There was a bank next door that had space to lease upstairs, attached to our space. Bruno came up with the brilliant idea that we'd open the adjoining wall. Now, any time you do major renovations like that you have to bring in a building inspector and get it all approved and get a permit. Bruno knew the process, so he made the application, and a representative from City Planning came round to see what we were proposing to do.

"Oh," he said. "You need another exit. You can't do this without putting in an exit."

"But there is an exit there — the side exit," I said. "And we've got the other two as well."

"Nope, sorry. You need another exit here."

I went home and told Bruno that the inspector was being very difficult. Bruno said, "Look, just go down and see the guy. Take him a bottle of wine or something."

"What? Are you asking me to bribe him?"

"No, no. Don't use that word. Just be nice. Just go and say that you think it looks okay, and you really need the space."

I couldn't imagine changing his mind, but when I went to see Mr. Building Inspector at City Hall I came up with my own strategy. While I sat waiting for him, I noticed a photo on his desk of two young girls, maybe 13 or 14 — pretty girls. I said, "Are these your children?"

He nodded, and I thought, Thank you, God. I said, "Well, for heaven's sake, you've got to bring them into my school. They're the perfect age for our Butterfly Connection program — and if they show an interest they might want to continue in our other programs."

He said, "Really? Do you think?"

I said, "Absolutely. You bring them in to see me. I'll have a chat with them. Because if they're interested we can definitely help each other here." He brought the girls in and they were indeed excited and wanted to start right away. I got my work permit, they got the course, and everything was peachy keen.

That incident unsettled me in a way. I saw that it probably went on all the time. People "helping" each other — that's how deals were done. I guess I was learning about business.

The Yonge Street location was fantastic. Perfect for my business. But we just kept expanding and soon we needed even more space. I leased another 1000 square feet down the street for the agency side of the business, but I quickly realized that separating the departments was not going to work out. The staff became disconnected. People need to work where there's constant support and supervision. So we needed to amalgamate the school and the agency.

The Importance of Great Employees

The business was becoming so popular that I could hardly keep up. My job became one of finding space and hiring and training staff. I was moving further and further away from the things that I loved to do — lecturing, teaching, hands-on day-to-day. As the president, you're forced into certain roles. The person at the top is the one who decides the how, who, where and when.

I'd always had a good instinct about people, and in business I developed a strong knack for choosing the best employees for particular positions. As I mentioned earlier, I had a lot of people who were really good at what they did so I'd make them managers of a department. They were responsible for training other teachers and contributed to our teachers' meetings and management meetings. I'd have a private meeting with each of them beforehand to see what they were going to say, and then I'd maybe make some suggestions: "What do you think of this? You know this area better than I do," and "Maybe you want to discuss that." But never telling them. At these meetings I would not say anything. I'd set the agenda, but I turned it over to them. It worked so well because everyone had their own responsibilities and a title. If you build up that confidence, you've got an employee for life. They're happy. They feel appreciated. My staff was very dedicated. I got much more out of them than if I came along and said what I wanted to be done. I tried hard to create a team atmosphere and be the kind of boss who practised what I preached: social graces, tact, sensitivity, personality, being positive and upbeat — and never letting ego get in the way.

Employees at every level need to feel needed. When I watch *Undercover Boss* on TV, I can relate very strongly because I know that top managers have to find a way to connect with people on the front line — the employees who are working every day and have two other jobs and are trying to keep it together and take it seriously and do a good job. I get emotional when I see these CEOs connect with their employees for the first time and show their appreciation. That's what it's all about — connecting. As I moved away from the teaching and got so busy running the company, I felt a little isolated. Yes, you're needed at the top, but you miss the kind of rewards you get when you're working with people on the front line and dealing with the public.

The key is to find the thing you're good at and give enough power to people who do their own thing better than you could do it. A story comes to mind that illustrates that philosophy — my day as a server at McDonald's. They used to have a Celebrity Day as a fundraiser for Ronald McDonald House. Well-known people were brought in to work the counter. If the customers bought the "celebrity" hamburger, the company donated a certain percentage of the sales. Now, I know my strengths, and "kitchen helper" is not one of them. There I am, behind the counter at McDonald's, smiling and happy to help out, but I'm not really into it. In fact, I'm terrible. There's a big line-up at my till, and I'm spilling the Cokes and the French fries are flying all over the counter and the floor. I was a wreck!

As I mentioned, it's just in my nature to do things as fast as I can. My thought process is, "Why make two trips for French fries when I can carry all three orders in one go?" I'm always looking for shortcuts. It doesn't always work.

Another problem — people weren't buying the special hamburger. Sure, we had lots of customers, but the point of the whole day was to raise funds. I had an idea. I said to the trainer who was responsible for making sure I didn't totally destroy the place, "I'll tell you what. I am not good at this. But I *am* very good at PR. I notice most of the people in this line-up aren't buying the special hamburger. You know why? You've got a sign up there, but people don't read signs. They're regulars here and they're just ordering what they normally order. They know it's Celebrity Day but they're not aware of what it's all about.

"We've got to raise more money than this," I said. "Let me try something, okay? Give me one hour in front of the counter instead of behind the counter." I went around the counter and very loudly said, "Excuse me, everyone. Just so you know, today is a special fundraising day. If you buy the Celebrity Hamburger, the money goes toward Ronald McDonald House. And I'm sure you want to support that." Almost immediately, sales doubled. I stayed where I belonged, much more effective than I'd been behind the counter! To this day I respect the front-line workers.

Know what you're good at and what you're not.

Myths and Realities

Back in the '60s and '70s, there was a lot of negativity about the modelling world. As I mentioned earlier, Bruce Johnston said "modelling was for tarts." And he was a very smart guy. But that attitude was typical — a lot of people thought models were pretty and dumb. In reality, many retired models went on to successful careers in business or acting or any number of fields. But in the early days of television, models were not even allowed to audition for TV commercials. Actors only! Today modelling experience is a bonus, because models are photogenic and are comfortable in front of the camera. How times have changed.

There was — and still is — a lot of misconception about the type of woman who becomes a model. Sometimes she has to walk on eggshells around other women. If she is outgoing and having fun at a social gathering, she might be branded a hussy. If she's quiet and shy, she's labelled a snob. Self-confident and proud of her beauty? Obviously a conceited b——!

A prevailing myth about the modelling industry was — and still is — that it was all high-paying glamour, cocktail parties, free designer clothes, all-night parties, chauffeur-driven limos and expensive gifts. While there may have been a little bit of that high-flying lifestyle for a few, the real picture was something else. The working models were probably exercising or sleeping!

This is an excerpt of an interview I gave to *Liberty* magazine:

Runway Modelling: You only see the runway aglitter with cool, every-hair-in-place fashion plates appearing on cue. But their unearthly perfection is achieved in a closet-sized cubicle for eight models to dress, undress, apply makeup, and fall into hysterics in. For they must be on cue. And heaven help them if they can't find the gold scatter pin for that quick-change number.

Catalogue photography: This is how that cute housedress you just ordered was photographed for your catalogue: The model mustn't move a muscle once the camera and lighting are set. For that's when the dresser and the hairstylist descend on her with scissors, pins, needles and tissue paper, designed to make the $2.98 housedress look like a $298 Balenciaga original. After she's been curled, pricked, pinned, sewn and stuffed, the photographer suddenly yells: "Now look like you've got the world by the tail!"

Showroom modelling: This takes place in the showroom of large dress manufacturers for the benefit of wholesale buyers from across Canada. Since buyers buy six months ahead, often the un-airconditioned showrooms boast an 80-degree temperature (and a 100-proof aura of smelly cigar smoke) while you model 40 winter suits and coats four times a day.

Despite these "hardships," there's a good reason a lot of women and men choose to pursue a career in modelling. It can open up a whole new world of interesting people and travel. But my philosophy about modelling, and particularly the training and education I offered at the school, was that it gives women that priceless, exhilarating feeling of being self-confident. It wasn't just about training to be a model, of course. It was about developing charm, self-assurance, and individual style. My greatest joy in running the school was being part of a woman's renaissance, helping her find her personal best. We stressed individualism. Letters like this one from a student meant so much to me: "When I first came here, I was alone and dejected. You've helped me to remake myself. My social life is great and I've been promoted twice at work. I've added it all up against what I paid for the course. It was like winning the lottery."

Model of the Year Awards Fashion Shows

The last class in the modelling course was the final exam, which I conducted personally. The incentive to pass was that students could participate in our annual Graduation Fashion Show. Maybe 60 percent would pass their first final exam and the rest would be assigned so many free practice classes to improve their walk, their hair, etc. It was my show and my name on the line so I wanted to be sure that everyone looked their absolute best. They were able to take as many final exams as they needed.

We had our first graduation in 1961 at the Lady Eaton estate in Toronto. A friend of mine, Janet Kinsella, whose husband struck it rich in real estate, had recently bought the estate. It had its own recital hall. Janet said one day, "Eleanor, why don't you have your Graduation Fashion Show at my place?"

Are you kidding me? The estate was magnificent and the perfect place for a glamorous event. The recital hall had its own stage (we rented a runway), and the room could accommodate about 300 seated guests. The home was so beautiful. It had a huge balcony that overlooked Mt. Pleasant Road. I was very grateful for that offer. All the tickets sold like hotcakes because everyone wanted to visit the Lady Eaton home. That 1961 show was incredible. It had a lot of the

Graduation, 1962. I'm in the middle of the front row. Janet Kinsella, with flowers, is beside me.

Graduation, 1963. I'm in the front row, with flowers.

Graduation, 1963, the Van Dyke twins

over-25s, the Dynasty group, who had gone on to the modelling course. They stole the show.

The graduations got bigger and bigger and soon we had to move into the Park Plaza Hotel, where we stayed for a few years. They got better and better, too. We did more complex choreography and sets, music, and it was great fun. We'd have ten different scenes: evening, day wear, swimwear, etc., and the models had to pick out their own outfits. They each wore two different outfits that had to be approved by me. They wore their own clothes, so there was never a need to buy anything special. By that time, they had to know what was their best look, their own individual style. I'd often bring in my own clothes for them to wear if I thought it was going to be a problem for anyone. It was a big event and very exciting for everyone involved. It's fun to look back on 30 years of shows and see how the clothes and the hairstyles have changed.

The graduation ceremonies grew into the Eleanor Fulcher Model of the Year Awards Fashion Show, which was enormous and which I absolutely loved producing. We'd have 300 to 500 students in the shows and an audience of about 3000 people. It was always sold out. Eventually we had to put on an afternoon show too, because there was such a demand for tickets. Even the afternoon show was a sell-out. We never made any money on these shows — it was very expensive to produce. I just wanted to break even, which we usually did.

The show was a huge production and very exciting. I'd make sure we had great music and a high-quality sound system, with Brian Master as musical director. We even had an original song, "Walking With My Head Up High." I wrote the lyrics: "I'm walking with my head up high; You told me I could do it; Do my best and get me through it…" It was a catchy tune and a big hit with the audience.

I held a contest to see who could design the best show scene. We'd have a series of scenes — maybe Paris, with a big picture of the Eiffel Tower, Cleopatra, or a nighttime setting with evening gowns. It made things interesting for the audience and was fun for the gradu-

Graduation, 1964 at the Park Plaza Hotel in Toronto. I'm in the middle of the front row.

Graduation 1965, Empress Room, Park Plaza Hotel in Toronto

ates. After the graduates were assigned their scene, each group was responsible for design, commentary, choreography, everything.

All the graduates had to help promote the show. Most of the students would attempt to get sponsors for the programs plus prize donations, and each year the prizes got bigger and better. The winner not only got a modelling contract, but those who came in first, second or third won many other valuable prizes. Many more of the graduates would get modelling contracts — that just went with the territory. The Model of the Year would get $10,000 in cash and prizes. We had six judges, all well known in the industry — top photographers, fashion coordinators and clients. They'd vote for their favourites in the female division, male division, kids division, and so on.

At the end of the show everyone would come on stage for the awards presentation. The excitement was unbelievable. I would stand stage left at the mic wearing a Canadian designer gown (I wore two gowns, one for opening the show and one for the closing ceremony). My vice president would gather the results from the judges and hand

Leili Pirso in a real showstopper

them to me on stage. I'd cue the music director: drum roll... Second Runner-up, First Runner-up, Winner! I would do this for each division. They would step forward and I'd present them with a trophy and they'd walk down the runway. At the end of the show everyone gathered on stage for a group photo plus individual photos that they could purchase from the photographer as a keepsake.

Many of the Eleanor Fulcher Model of the Year winners became very successful. It didn't hurt that they got great press. Our show had become quite famous, so with press coverage on TV, radio, newspapers and magazines, the models' careers were launched.

So much work and preparation went into these shows. I'd be relieved and exhausted at the cocktail party afterwards. A friend and business associate, Barbara Leimbrock, reminded me recently that as soon as the show was over, I lost my voice — every year. The girls would laugh! It was like I was running on empty near the end, going on

ELEANOR FULCHER PRESENTS

Eleanor Fulcher Presents, 1986. Our Dynasty ladies

nerves and all that adrenalin, and the minute I could relax and the show was over — boom, no voice. My dear friend Joan McCormick Frankel sat me down after one show and said, "Eleanor, you can't do everything — it's too big. When you come on stage to address the audience it's like you've completed the four-minute mile — out of breath and screechy. You need to make an entrance — calm, collected, glamorous — to set the right mood." She was right. It was too big for me to do it all. So I went searching for a choreographer to replace myself.

I tried two different choreographers but they weren't right because they always turned it over to me as soon as I questioned anything. "Well, what do you want us to do, Eleanor?" Wrong answer. I don't want someone who's always deferring to me; that's not why I hired them. I wanted someone to say, "If you don't like that, then I have five other ideas we can use. Here they are — I know you'll be happy with one of them." I wanted them to fight for their territory.

Finally, I found the person I'd been hoping for: Andy Body, an accomplished choreographer of international fame. He was handsome, charming and self-assured. His credentials were incredible. We negotiated and I hired him. During rehearsal of his first show with me, I made the mistake of stepping on his toes, asking him to change this and that and wondering aloud, "Shouldn't they enter stage left?" My past experience with choreographers had left me very apprehensive. He finally blew up at me in front of everyone. "Who the f— is choreographing this show — you or me?" I loved it. I just broke up and started laughing. This is the person I wanted. He was ballsy, he was in control and he was a nervous wreck — just like I'd

Makeup demonstration at the Lady Eaton estate, 1961. That's me on the left, and George Abbott and Shirley Kohl

been before every show! He was the first person that didn't look at me and say, "What do you think of this, Eleanor?" He took charge. Every year since that time Andy writes on his Christmas card, "Who the f— is choreographing this show, you or me?" which still breaks me up. He's so funny, he could be a stand-up comedian. And he was a great choreographer. He cared deeply about the show and everyone knew he cared and they respected his directions. At last I could relax and focus on my job as emcee. What a relief. Andy did my shows for ten years until I sold the business. We're still very close friends.

As soon as one show was over, we started planning for the next one. I'd book a year ahead in large hotels with the proper stage facilities. We booked different Toronto venues such as the Park Plaza, Royal York, Exhibition Place, Harbour Castle Hilton and Inn on the Park.

My vice-president Joanne Benham, Andy Body, and me.

I hired a professional to videotape the whole show, two-and-a-half hours or so, and edit it down to 15 or 20 minutes of highlights. We used the film as a sales tool for prospective students. At their first appointment we'd seat them in a small, dark room and we'd start the film, with my voice-over commentary. It was very exciting to watch. By the time they viewed the film and met with a counsellor, all they wanted to know was how much, when's the next show, and when can I start?

Publicity and Public Relations

Advertising was very expensive — getting publicity was much more economical. I had to be creative when it came to PR, and because of my advertising background I think I was good at it. I'd always enjoyed marketing and promotion, and when it came to promoting my own business, I went all out.

I had a full-time PR department. I needed to let people know the school and agency existed, and to get my name known as the go-to person on beauty and fashion. I wanted to be the spokesperson for our industry, and I was. The media anointed me as the person to contact if you wanted to get the real lowdown about what was going on. I knew speaking openly and honestly would always hold me in good stead with the media.

Once during a very bad economic time I sent out a press release saying, "The martini lunches are over," and did that strike a chord! I was getting calls from every news medium across Canada that wanted my comments.

We sent out press releases whenever we thought something or someone was newsworthy. We had a support system in place for radio, print and TV — all great exposure. The media would call me for my opinion or for appearances, and I'd drop everything and discuss it over the phone or taxi down for a quick interview. I instructed the staff that whenever they got a call from the media they had to track me down. They always knew where to reach me.

One day Betty Kennedy decided to do a radio broadcast about modelling and wanted to get the real scoop about the industry. She had a personal interest because at breakfast that morning her daughter had expressed some interest in modelling. That same morning her PR guy phoned our school at 10:50 a.m. to request an interview with me. Betty's program went live at 12 o'clock. My staff knew I was at my Globetrotters Investment Club meeting (a group of 18 women who met once a month), and one of them phoned me. "Betty Kennedy wants to interview you at noon. The topic is 13-year-olds modelling."

"Tell her I'll be there." The media is very "now." I took a cab down to the studio and was on with Betty Kennedy at 12 o'clock. My investment club meeting was still in progress so they all listened to the live radio program. There I was on the radio when less than an hour ago I'd been at the meeting. That's the sort of thing that I would be ready to do in a minute. Ready for anything!

The media came to rely on me as a valuable resource for our industry. The newspapers would ask me to provide them with photos of models in particular fashion attire. I had an incredible library of photos — headshots, composite, before-and-after, etc. This saved the newspaper or magazine the inconvenience of having to send a photographer and I got a credit line for the picture: "Photo courtesy of Eleanor Fulcher Agency."

The PR people would book me to give lectures, too. I had finally come to love public speaking. Any time I could talk about any phase of the business I was quite happy. I gave talks to high school students, York University Entrepreneurs Club, large companies, women's groups. It was a highly interesting industry and I had a lot of experiences to share, so these talks were in demand.

I had appearances on several TV shows such as *You're Beautiful* with Micki Moore. Before-and-after shots were always a big hit. I'd show photos and talk about the transformations, or we'd just chat about the industry: what's hot, what's not, what's good in makeup, what's good in fashion, what's happening in the modelling industry. I got to know and like many of the hosts and hostesses of these shows.

Elwy Yost, who hosted the popular *Saturday Night at the Movies* for TVOntario, came to our school to film some of the models on the runway. He was critiquing the movie *Funny Face* with Audrey Hepburn and Fred Astaire, and wanted to interview me and show what the models went through and get some real background on the industry. He was a great guy. I loved talking to him about movies; he was so knowledgeable. I miss him.

I was asked to judge a lot of beauty contests, including Miss World Canada, though most were on a smaller scale. One year, there was to be a beauty contest held in a small town in Ontario, a very picturesque little town that I'd never been to before, so I thought, What the heck, this will be fun.

The competition was held in a huge old barn-like stadium. About 20 girls from neighbouring towns were competing. I was the only judge — the mayor had backed out (smart mayor). As each contestant was introduced, the audience made it known through applause and screaming who was their choice — their hometown girl. I felt rather sorry for the other contestants. However, I was not going to be intimidated — after all, I'm the professional, right!

It was quite obvious to me who the winner was, and it wasn't the hometown girl. A beautiful girl from a different town was head and shoulders above anybody else in terms of poise, personality and appearance. The big moment came — drum roll, a hushed audience — and I announced her as the winner. There was dead, icy silence. You could almost feel the crowd's disapproval and disappointment. Oh-oh, I thought, I'm in trouble.

I had to think on my feet — fast — and then I got an idea. "Ladies and gentlemen, before I continue and name the runners-up, let me explain that I employ generally accepted universal judging procedures." And I went on and on about this elaborate system whereby the girls got so many points for swimsuit, so many points for makeup, hair, nails, skin tone, this many points for speech, poise and so on. Occasionally, for effect, I'd pretend to study my notes, which had nothing to do with a judging system. "And the girl who came in second by the slightest fraction of a point is...Miss "(their local girl)." The place erupted, everyone screaming and yelling their approval. I went down the list of runners-up but by then nothing mattered.

Phew! I quickly walked off the stage, relieved that everyone seemed happy, but then I was met by all these local journalists — at least ten of them.

"Miss Fulcher, could we please have copies of those judging sheets? We'd like to report those judging procedures you used; it's very interesting and I think our readers would like to see how it all works." Oh.

There were no judging sheets, no system, no procedures, no universal standards. Clutching my notes to my chest, I said, "Oh yes, certainly. Um, I left something backstage so if you'll just give me a minute, I'll be right back." I went backstage, found an exit, almost ran to my car, and took off.

To top off the evening, I got lost. I had driven out of the parking lot so fast I had no idea which way I was headed. Plus I was almost out of gas. It was pitch black on these little country roads; quite scary. I pulled over and got out, and stuck out my thumb when I saw a car coming — and it stopped! It was an old couple in what looked

In 1961, the Eleanor Fulcher School of Beauty was featured in *Liberty* magazine.

We often received good press. This was in the *Toronto Sun*, 1977.

Toronto Daily Star, 1968. The caption was: Eleanor Fulcher chats with her secretary in her executive offices. The young woman, who has succeeded in business by really trying, says it is sometimes lonely in the executive suite. Miss Fulcher believes the successful woman can be feminine. [Photo credit: Norm James]

like a Model T Ford — I'd never seen a car like it — and when I told them I was running out of gas they offered to escort me to a gas station to make sure I was okay. Bless them. Very sweet people. In spite of everything that happened that day I was left with a positive feeling at the end of the day thanks to that delightful old couple. However, I never judged another contest.

I would frequently emcee for a good cause, such as the *Toronto Sun*'s Working Women Fashion Seminar at Simpson's Arcadian Court in 1981. It was a sign of the times — advising women how to dress for success at the office. Another time, I organized a fashion show for the wives of delegates of the Automotive Transport Asso-

LIFE/CLASSIFIED

Top women: Kingston Penitentiary warden Mary Dawson, modelling agency head Eleanor Fulcher and lawyer Jane Harvey discuss road to success

Hard work, good sense of humor keys to success, top women advise

Toronto Star, 1984

It's painless fashion for agent

Smart style
Ellen Bot

Toronto model agent Eleanor Fulcher used to suffer for fashion and beauty. "When I modelled in the '50s, I wore waist-cinchers, padded bras and tight turban hats," she says. "I was only 17 but I looked 10 years older." Fulcher, now 50 and relaxed about her sense of style, celebrates the 20th anniversary of her modelling agency and school this year.

Here are her fashion and beauty philosophies:

Skin care: "When I modelled, people didn't care about their skin. They were more interested in makeup," she says. Fulcher has developed her own line of skin-care products, which are sold at her Bathurst and Christie Sts. headquarters.

In the morning, she uses her body lotion, toner and rich moisturizer. At night she puts on Float Away cleanser, massages her face and rinses with 30 splashes of water. Every two weeks, she "paints" on a mint mask facial.

Makeup: "Today we have women who are beautiful with or without makeup," says Fulcher, citing Sophia Loren and Jane Fonda as examples. She wears the same makeup for every occasion but accentuates her eyes for elegant evenings. She dislikes wearing foundation. "As soon as I get a light tan, I don't wear it."

Hair: Fulcher bleached her dark auburn hair at age 18. "I wanted to see if blondes had more fun." Her first attempt at becoming blonde was disastrous. "The hairdresser left the color on too long." Fortunately, she had fashion on her side. "Everyone wore hats in the '50s, so I went to modelling jobs with my head covered. I enjoyed being a blonde, but to this day my scalp is ruined from the bleach."

Fashion: "I'm glad that I was a model during the glamorous period. We looked like models in those days. Today girls come to their bookings dressed in blue jeans." She remembers wearing wide crinolines, mink stoles and strapless gowns in the '50s.

"I'm more confident about fashion today. Before I wouldn't dare to wear anything different." Fulcher looks back at the mini-skirt madness of the '60s. "We all were torn whether it suited us or not. Women rebelled after that."

Diet: "A toned 133 pounds is my best weight now," says Fulcher, who is 5 feet 7 inches. She weighed 118 pounds when she was a model. "Older women look better with a extra five pounds. It plumps up the skin."

Eleanor Fulcher: Model agent is glad models don't have to suffer for fashion any more. She says she used to wear waist-cinchers, padded bras and tight turban hats when she modelled in the '50s.

Toronto Star, 1985

ciation, who were having their convention at the Royal York Hotel. They were housewives, but for that day they were turned into glamorous models with tips on makeup, fashion, walking, etc. It was a big hit. After the convention, I received a letter from one of the women from Manitoba. "I thought you'd like to know," she wrote, "my husband told me, 'Mother, you were gorgeous. Never thought there was that much life in the old horse yet.' (From him, this was a compliment.) He hasn't stopped pulling out chairs for me and lighting my cigarettes. Our children think Toronto worked real magic in turning Dad into a regular gentleman." I loved working with these women. We had so much fun.

Because of all the PR my name became quite well known and I was privileged to be booked for some pretty exciting events such as Expo '67 in Montreal, where I was hired to train the hosts and hostesses who worked at the Ontario Pavilion. Most of that experience is a blur because I was so busy I hardly had time to see any of it. The one incident I remember clearly is sitting near the back of the plane en route to Montreal. I got a horrible attack of claustrophobia. I had to control it until the plane landed, at which point I leapt to my feet, grabbed my two makeup kits, and pushed my way to the front of the plane with everyone yelling at me. Since then, I only sit near the front of any plane and take some Gravol to help me relax. Phobias can be very inconvenient.

Fulcher's Line Beauty Columns

Starting in 1983, I published a beauty column in the *Toronto Sun*, which turned out to be fabulous publicity. I first got the idea because over the years I had written so many teaching manuals on so many subjects that it seemed natural that some of this information should be shared.

A New You in the New Year

Toronto Sun announcement about Fulcher's Line

If there is anyone in Toronto who knows fashion, beauty and grooming, it's Eleanor Fulcher. As president of Eleanor Fulcher Ltd., a multi-faceted company which includes a self-improvement and modeling school and an agency for many of Toronto's top models, her career for the past twenty years has been devoted to women's needs. Now she is bringing her vast knowledge and experience to Lifestyle readers of the Toronto Sun. Beginning tomorrow, watch for Eleanor Fulcher's tips on beauty and grooming in Imagination. You won't have to imagine a new you much longer.

The little paper that grew

My very dear friend and journalist and one of our part-time teachers, Joan McCormick Frankel, said that she'd be interested in working with me to pull all the information together, and we prepared some sample columns. The *Toronto Sun* had recently been launched and Doug Creighton, the founder, loved the idea of Fulcher's Line after I showed him the samples. (Incidentally, I knew his wife, Marilyn, from our Investment Club.) He even offered to pay me $200 per column. I gave Joan the $200 for every column, and we had fun discussing and dissecting all the information.

The column was highly successful and ran for three years — more than 150 columns. Most of the information is still applicable today, three decades later. Some of the titles of the columns were Bargain-Basement Beauty Tips; Breaking the Sound Barrier — Your Voice; First-Aid for Flabby Fannies; Energy — Better Than Beauty; Executive Suite Beauty Basics.

Doug Creighton and me at a Globetrotters Investment Club annual dinner.

In 1987, through my association with the International Modeling and Talent Association, one of the Fulcher's Line columns was chosen as the foreword to *How to Become a Professional Model*, a book with worldwide distribution by American author Jon Addams. It sums up my views about what it takes.

SO YOU WANT TO BE A MODEL

BY ELEANOR FULCHER

So you want to be a model? Judging from the number of letters I receive, there are scads of aspiring models, age nine to 90.

This widespread interest is not too unusual, when you see 13-year olds on the covers of Vogue and Bazaar, and watch galvanized grannies on the tube hawking everything from flea and tick collars to go-with-the-floor pens. What are your chances?

Basically, there are two major areas of modelling: commercial (print and television, trade shows, promotions, etc.) and high fashion (fashion photography, runway modelling, etc.). Generally, a prime candidate for high fashion would be 5'8" and taller, size 6 or 8; photogenic. Notice I did not say beautiful. These would be basic guidelines rather than iron-clad rules, because we have all learned that there are exceptions to rules!

Successful models are often made, not born. While there is no doubt that beauty is a bonus, and good bone structure, good carriage and a good figure are great assets, even more are the know-how and certain intangible factors: determination, self-discipline, energy and enthusiasm.

Through years of experience in training models, I have discovered that often those with the greatest basic potentials are also those who never make it to the finish line. Sometimes the problem is laziness or lack of commitment. Other girls with far less going for them prove to be the long distance runners with the stamina and staying power and sheer will to succeed. They apply themselves to learning their craft; they master the makeup techniques that create beauty; they learn how to move to display clothes; they study photo angles; they tone their bodies and do exercises to stay supple and graceful.

They have the self-discipline to stay on a nutrition regimen that will keep figure, hair and nails in peak condition. Their calories have to count to keep energy high and bodies lean. If you have wondered why models need to be thin, the camera adds ten mean pounds! That means to look 120 you have to weigh 110!

Experience is also a great teacher. If you compare pictures of a model at the start of her career, with photos taken five years later, after she has hit her stride, you will be amazed at the changes. Not older, just better!

You learn by doing, by comparing notes and observing the styles of other professional models. You study your own photos and commercials to see where you can improve. You experiment with different looks to increase your versatility and marketability so that you can bring something new and different to each assignment. It is challenging, exhilarating and often hard work!

Oddly enough, models are rarely conceited; they are far too aware of their flaws. Lauren Hutton talks objectively of her "banana nose" and the gap between her teeth. Ruthless self-appraisal is the key to effective self-projection. Many a model is matter-of-fact about problem hair, closeset eyes, a square jaw or short-waist. Knowledge is power, especially in the modelling profession. Models learn to dazzle you with their assets; they camouflage the flaws or flaunt them as a trademark.

When it comes to commercial modelling, the rule book goes out the window — no physical limits in terms of age, size, shape, or voice quality. It hinges entirely on what type is needed to sell the product in question — a freckle-faced kid, a two-ton Tessie, a cushiony grandmother. Pretty is not necessary — sometimes pretty is a problem. To establish credibility a sponsor or advertiser needs believable people to do the washing, unplug the drain, clean the oven and check glasses for spots. It is a case of bless 'em all — the long and the short and the tall — and the babies, dogs, cats and koala bears…

As with high fashion modelling, once you have learned the skills, success or failure is squarely up to you. Nothing comes on a silver platter. This is perhaps where the individual used to pursuing goals has the advantages, because as with all things in life, the prize goes to the doer, not the dreamer.

— ELEANOR FULCHER
President of Eleanor Fulcher Model School
and Agency, Toronto, Canada.

Here are a few more Fulcher's Line columns:

November 26, 1981

THE DEFINITION OF A LADY

Is being a "lady" outmoded? Are good manners really passé? Let's define our terms here, because a lot of women find the word "lady" offensive. If lady means someone born to title, wealth or position — or if it means a passive, spineless, smarmy goody-two-shoes — then good riddance! But if it means (by my definition) a woman who is gracious, courteous, considerate and thoughtful of others — a woman who meets life head-on with a smile in her voice and one on her face — then I'd say the "lady" is a keeper. (And we'd better protect the species because it's in danger of becoming extinct.)

It's good to have our consciousness raised, to recognize no limits in terms of career options. Yes — we have a right to equal pay for equal work. Certainly we should become more self-sufficient. Decidedly, we should be more vocal in decision-making at all levels. But we still can keep the qualities I attribute to a lady. We can be strong, purposeful and resolute, but do we have to be rude? Strong convictions don't have to equate to strong language. High decibel delivery — whether at home, in the classroom, or on the job — simply gets tuned out. We can be competent and competitive without being coarse. Maybe in our effort to establish equality we've been overcompensating. Like the golfer who's trying to correct a splice, we've developed a hook.

Ladies come in all shapes and sizes, young and old, rich and poor, with grade-school education or PhDs. A lady is the Queen Mum; a lady is the waitress who says good morning with a smile; a lady is the school-girl who gives up her seat on the bus to a senior citizen. A lady is the high-powered executive who shows grace under pressure; a lady is also the woman who still says please and thank you.

Women who assume an adversary stance on every issue start getting paranoid. Nothing is going to take advantage of them. Those who might not be too pushy in any eyeball-to-eyeball confrontation often vent their hostility on telephone canvassers, department store switchboard operators and nurse-receptionists. Behind the wheel of a car they come on like Attila the Hun. They show less driver courtesy than any man; they offer no quarter to anyone who tries to change lanes or hang a left.

Woman power is very special and as women move into more and more key positions we'll wield more and more influence. We will be in a position to participate in establishing standards and setting the climate for effective interaction. Let's make sure that woman power is positive power. Let's root for the woman who makes her mark and her point with grace and finesse — the lady.

June 4, 1981

SMART IDEAS FOR SAVVY SHOPPERS

Are you a savvy shopper when it comes to clothes? It's not difficult to learn to "shop smart," but first you have to do your homework.

Start by taking inventory of the clothes you already own for the current season. It's your best guarantee for achieving an integrated wardrobe. Lay them out on the bed, try them all on for fit and condition. Also try pairing things up differently. Suit jackets can team up with other skirts and slacks for new looks. Dresses look different with a blazer or weskit on top. Too-tight shirts can be worn unbuttoned over T-shirts, leotards, halter-tops or camisoles. Once you get the hang of it, you'll be amazed at the versatility of the clothes you already own.

LIST ALL the "keepers" in categories in a small notebook. If there is any spare fabric on a dress, skirt, etc. (an over-generous seam allowance or leftovers from a hemline "hike"), snip off a piece and staple it into the book. It's a big help in choosing mix-and-match additions to your wardrobe. Even colour matches from a fashion magazine will do the trick.

NEXT MOVE: Give some thought to defining your fashion image — i.e. classic, sporty, tailored, hard chic, soft chic, etc. The definition ideally should co-ordinate your look and your personality or you'll be sending out false signals.

Now, list your range of activities and interests. No point in investing in another cocktail dress if it won't be seeing service. This exercise will help you focus on your real needs and reduce the risk of impulse buying.

Here are some other sure-fire guidelines for the savvy shopper:

SHOP MID-MOOD: If you're too "up," everything will look sensational until you get it home. If you're too down, you'll be low on sales resistance and an easy prey.

SEASONLESS: Look for year-round or seasonless clothes — lightweight woollens, silks or silky looks, twills, lightweight jerseys and knits. By adding or subtracting cardigans, jackets or coats, you'll be able to get at least spring/fall/winter mileage from the same outfits.

SIMPLICITY: Shop for simple lines. It's good economy and good fashion because you can dress up or down and make a personal statement with accessories.

AVOID FADS: Don't invest heavily in fad fashions. They have a short, short lifespan. Indulge occasionally but in an inexpensive item.

SHOP FOR QUALITY and develop an eagle eye. Check for: A decent (half an inch) seam allowance; seams bound or overcast; lining through hip and fanny area of skirts and slacks; buttons that do up easily; zippers that slide smoothly; seams that don't pucker; seams that line up. Crumple a little of the fabric in your hand and let go. If it wrinkles you'll look like an unmade bed by mid-day!

COLOURS: Limit your colour range. Choose important pieces in basic colours. Remember basic needn't be black. It can be grey, taupe, navy, beige, camel, white, brown. Other harmonizing colours can be introduced in secondary pieces — shirts, sweaters, or in accessories — scarves, belts, etc. Always check out colours in natural light. In-store lighting alters shades somewhat.

USE A MIRROR: Check out every potential purchase in a three-way mirror to get the whole story.

SHOP "FIT," not size. Manufacturers' sizing is not standard and tight clothes are never flattering.

FINALLY, ask yourself these questions: Does it make me look good? Does it make me feel good? Does it suit my lifestyle? If the answers are yes and you can afford it, grab it — it's a winner.

We would mix up the "formula" for the Fulcher's Line column to keep it fresh. Sometimes it would be a meat-and-potatoes piece covering things like how-to's of makeup application, grooming, etc. Then there was the popular Mailbag, a question-and-answer column. The Zingers were slightly offbeat things like inflation-beater beauty tips, or preparing your knees for the return of the miniskirt. And finally the Special Interest columns, which might cover something like how to update your makeup for a return to the workforce, or makeup tips to boost the morale of senior citizens. Working with Joan on these columns was fun, and it sure kept the name front and centre.

Journal of a Busy Life

I recently came across some old journals and appointment books. I don't know how I found time for it all! Here's just a sample from 1980.

Bruno, me, Joan Sutton and her husband Oscar Straus

Dinner at Winston's (with Doug Creighton and Joan Sutton, to celebrate my 20 years in business. Joan was a highly successful journalist who wrote the Sutton's Place column for the *Toronto Sun*. We were very close friends and still are.)

Meeting with Tom Reynolds (Tom resurrected the Miss Canada pageant. It had lain dormant for many years because someone had badly managed it into bankruptcy. I worked with Tom for three or four years to rebuild its image. He eventually sold the rights to CFTO for mega bucks and it became one of their most popular TV shows.)

Showcase class (This was a class where I talked to the students about their Showcase at the end of the modelling course. The Showcase was a smaller show that we did on the premises as preparation for the much larger Graduation Show at the hotel, which ultimately grew into the Eleanor Fulcher Model of the Year Awards Fashion Show.)

Globetrotters meeting (My investment group — 18 great ladies, 33 years of meetings, keeping abreast of the money market.)

Unique Lives Luncheon (When internationally known personalities came to Toronto to speak at this event, we provided models as the hostesses. I would receive two guest passes for the event. At the pre-luncheon cocktail party for the head-table guests we would have our photos taken with these famous speakers, such as top CEOs, politicians, etc. Very interesting. At one luncheon I was seated next to four young Coca-Cola executives. They told me there was going to be a big announcement the next day — the "New Coke." They were changing the formula of Coca-Cola! I was stunned! I lambasted them. It wasn't just the taste; it's the history. For instance, during World War I, hundreds of cases of Coke were shipped to the troops, to cheer them up and remind them of what they were fighting for. Changing Coke? I was livid. This was personal. Well, we all know the outcome of that story. In 79 days they brought back Coke Classic. The New Coke was probably one of the biggest blunders in marketing history. A funny coincidence: the cover of a 2013 Coke calendar has a famous poster of a model named Lillian Patterson. She was 18 at the time, 1933, and photographed with Ontario's Scarborough Bluffs in the background. It's a classic pose from the golden age of Coke advertisements. Now, what makes this noteworthy is that Coke model is Lillian Patterson, the mother of my friend Cathy Richardson's son-in-law Peter Langer! Small world.

Dentist (Dr. Purves, the best dentist in the world)

Meeting with VP Joanne Benham (our weekly management meeting)

The model in this 1933 Coke poster was Lillian Patterson, whose son, Peter Langer, provided me with the photo [inset] taken around the same time as the ad was released.

Models Workshop (We'd have regular workshops for our professional models to review what was happening and keep them up to date on the latest hair and makeup trends, new clients, and so on.)

Meeting with Joan McCormick (regarding *Sun* columns)

Immigration, Roseanne (working to get my housekeeper Landed Immigrant status)

Marketing Awards (an annual dinner for advertisers)

Steve Bodri (Steve was in charge of the Eleanor Fulcher Spa construction.)

Call Wolfgang in Berlin (my friend who bought a half-ownership in 791 St. Clair)

Brian Master (musical director for our Model of the Year shows — did he ever know his music!)

Francesca (a Canadian designer just starting out who designed some of my clothes)

Lunch at Fenton's (my favourite restaurant at the time)

Upper Canada College Music Festival (where my son, Marcus, went to school)

Bayview Glen graduation (My daughter, Angela, was graduating from Grade 8.)

Leave for Cape Cod (family vacation with Angela, Marcus and Bruno and our friends the Ross family)

Student model auditions (opportunity for students to be booked in the Agency's Student Model Division for experience)

Brig re posters (Brig was my graphic artist — and a creative genius. She really understood my business and captured what we represented. She became a single mom — with no idea how to raise a child. I offered to look after her two-year-old son for a

I had the opportunity to meet many famous personalities. This is Colin Powell, U.S. Secretary of State, in May 1996, and Traute Siebert, Jesse Jackson and me in October 1991.

week when Brig went to California on a job. My housekeeper/
nanny and I could not get this child to eat anything. Brig had
fed him only cream puffs! By the second day I was frantic and
took the little boy to Dr. Laski, our family pediatrician, who
was quite famous. He told me, if the child would not eat, to
throw the food in the garbage, right in front of him! I had to
follow his instructions even though it killed me. By the second
day, after throwing out only two meals, the boy grabbed the
food when I went to throw it out — "No no! I eat!" — and I
had no more problems.)

Gordon Hay studios (Gordon Hay was a top fashion photographer. He and George Abbott produced a book called *100
Women of Canada* in which I was included.)

Dancercize (I made time for dancercize!)

Meeting — Own TV show (At one point I contemplated doing a
weekly TV show but decided it would be too time consuming.)

One of Brig's
illustrations

Rothmans speech (Andy Body's partner, Alan Hanlon, was in charge of all Rothmans promotions, and he hired me to speak about Canadian models, a subject about which I was passionate.)

I've always been busy (and still am). Recently I found my diary from 1954. Lots of dating — lunch, dinner, dancing till the wee hours — when did I ever sleep?

Once, while I was living on Caroline Avenue with my parents, the phone rang. My mother answered the phone. (I was upstairs.) "Is this David?" she said.

"No..."

"Oh — John?"

"Uh, no...."

"Stan?" And she went on, guessing four different names! The poor guy on the other end of the phone was probably saying to himself, "Oh. I thought Eleanor liked me."

Later I barked, "Mother! What were you thinking?"

She said, "I don't know. I've met so many I guess I got confused."

My mother loved meeting my dates. She'd sit them down in the kitchen and treat them like they were already members of the family. I'd take her aside afterwards and say, "Mother, don't get too cozy!" I didn't want them to think they were there to meet the parents and all that implies.

I read these journals and diaries now and wonder how I did it. But what fun we had!

The dating scene has changed dramatically. Do today's young men treat young women with flowers, romantic dinners and dancing? I don't think so. More likely they'd send a text message to meet them somewhere. When I was dating we'd often go out for dinner and dancing. I had three special male friends — I liked to call them

Mel and Norma Morassutti at my 40th birthday at Maxwell's Plum in Toronto

the Three Musketeers: Angelo, Rudy and Mel. They were so much fun, and doing very well in business. They would call me at work around 8 p.m. "We feel like dinner and dancing. Get a couple of girls and we'll pick you up at 9:30 outside Walter Thornton's." And there they'd be — three Cadillac convertibles lined up. I had no trouble convincing two employees to join me. They were all single and beautiful and loved a special evening of dinner and dancing — with no expectations! They knew the Three Musketeers were gentlemen. Mel Morassutti became a dear, lifelong friend along with his lovely wife, Norma, and later became godfather to my daughter, Angela. We did have fun!

Transformations

One year the government approached me to train three transsexuals who had had sex change operations. In the 1970s, that was almost unheard of. The government sponsored our program to aid the men in their changeover. We taught them how to care for their skin, learn makeup, hair, clothes, nails, walk and mannerisms — the whole program. They loved it. It's who they were. All they needed was training, practice and acceptance. We were happy to help. Of course, in the beauty and fashion industry there are lots of gay men, so that was not unusual, but this was different. This was new. I told my teaching staff, "We've got to all be comfortable with this. These are women trapped in male bodies." They were great students because they so desperately wanted to fit into their new role. And grateful that at last people understood.

People and Personalities

The Agency and School were growing, but the School was really where my heart was. I wasn't thrilled with many of the people we had to deal with in the Agency — not in the '60s and '70s. There were too many pompous phonies with huge egos. Fashion editors, agents, some clients — they wore their positions on their sleeves and you never got to know the real person. The attitude was: I'm here and you're not, and I call the tune because I'm either going to book your models and talent or I'm not. They owned their own little worlds and made themselves gods or goddesses.

I was at a cocktail party once for owners of model schools and agencies, and there was a new agent schmoozing everybody he could corner. I overheard someone ask him what he did and he replied, "I'm in the flesh-peddling business." What? This guy knew nothing about our field; had absolutely no experience. He thought he'd just sign some beautiful girls and book them.

I turned to him and looked him in the eye. "Is that what you think this business is? Flesh peddling. Really?"

He looked suitably chagrined. "Oh, no no, I didn't mean that."

It was jerks like him that gave the industry a bad name. Guys who didn't respect the industry and didn't care about the models. They figured it was an easy way to make money and be around beautiful women.

Others saw the success of my agency and figured they could take away some of my business, usually unethically. Once, one of my staff came to me and said, "Eleanor, do you know that there are two models standing outside our entrance handing out flyers for another school and agency?"

I said, "Really. Outside our door." I went outside, and here are these two lovely girls standing outside our front door, handing out flyers to our students advertising this other school and agency. I said, "Girls, this is beneath you. You do not have to do this. I would never ask any of our models to do something so degrading as to stand outside a competitor's place of business. I presume you're being very well paid! Now, if you'd like to leave your agency and join us, I promise you will never have to do a thing like this again. Now please go away. Just tell your agency you refuse to do this. And if you want to join us, give me a call." They were very upset, and said they were so sorry and they hadn't wanted to do it. It was an assignment. They left.

One year I was attending the annual convention of the International Modeling and Talent Association in New York. I always took an employee to assist in directing our models, so that year I took Betty-Jean Talbot — BJ we called her.

During these conventions, which were well attended with at least 1500 people, a fashion guru walked around observing everyone. On the final day of the convention, he presented an award to the individual he thought had exceptional style sense. Almost everyone looked great. For example, there were girls from Texas with unlimited budgets wearing original designer clothes. On the last day of the convention there was great excitement as this fashion expert with great fanfare announced the winner with the greatest fashion look. "And the winner is…Betty-Jean Talbot from Toronto, Canada!" BJ walked up on stage wearing a little black dress, very simple, with her perfect makeup and perfect hair, simple jewelry, and perfectly poised. It was a lovely moment. I was so proud of her.

Fast-forward a few months. BJ was a single mom with two children, who had only discovered she was pregnant — with twins — after she'd left her husband. Now, this was a woman who looked like she had it all. She was perfect. She always looked totally put together. But she confessed to me one night, "Eleanor, I nearly fainted when they called my name that night at the convention. You know that dress I wore? It cost me $8. I have never spent more than $10 on a dress." (Her husband wasn't paying any support at that time and she was very strapped financially.)

My friend BJ Talbot

I said, "Pardon?"

She said, "It's true. I buy all my clothes at second-hand stores."

The major lesson learned from her winning that award: style is not a price tag! It's an overall look — makeup, hair, figure, poise and clothes sense. You don't have to spend a fortune to look great. Simplicity, a good, well-trained eye for detail, and confidence. I encourage women to not spend more than their budgets allow — and to be happy when they discover great bargains. I know many women who are great shoppers and never pay full retail — they wait for the sales. And many slightly used fashion stores have incredible one-of-a-kind outfits, often designer labels and often never worn. So if you want to always be in style but lack the budget, look around. There are lots of options.

Back to BJ. She told me she did all her own electrical and plumbing work, learning from instruction manuals! The resourcefulness of that woman! BJ had won a coveted job at CBC when Ross McLean hired her for the TV program *701* over hundreds of other candidates when Joyce Davidson left. But one day, right in the middle of an interview with some intellectual who was spouting all these abstract ideas while she's attempting to know what he's talking about, she just got up and walked out without completing the interview. She had had enough of the pressure and the constant criticism — people telling her what to do and what not to do — not to mention difficult guests. She just couldn't handle the constant stress of the job while raising four children. Somehow she coped, with very little help. We were close friends and business associates. Later she was my maid of honour at my wedding. Sadly, she died in her early fifties of lung cancer. She had been addicted to cigarettes. Such a loss. We salute you, BJ.

Running a fast-growing business requires well-trained, dedicated and loyal employees. Having performed virtually every task myself

Some of the
staff in my first
office

Staff, 1962

Our 15th Anniversary with some of the original staff

A Very Merry Christmas from all of us

Staff Christmas photo at 667 Yonge Street, Toronto

Staff, December 1991

at some point, I had a lot of appreciation — and admiration — for all of them, no matter what level they were at in the company. I took care of them, paying them fairly and offering good benefits, a group insurance plan, and many fun get-togethers to allow everyone to unwind. I like to think that ours was a good place to work. I never had a big staff turnover, which is important. If you're good to your employees, they'll stay with you.

When I consider the number of people I hired over the years, it's astonishing that I didn't get more bad apples than I did. When that happened, it was more than likely the result of not paying attention to my gut instincts. For instance, there was the time when I needed a sales manager and relied on the advice of a headhunter who told me I needed a man for that job. Okay, I thought, he's the expert. He screened many applicants and settled on a man from Ottawa who seemed to have the necessary qualifications and was willing to move to Toronto. So I hired him.

In 1990, we celebrated 30 years in business! A group of us took a bus up to the Spa for the day, reminisced, drank wine, went out to dinner in Gravenhurst, and had a lot of fun. At one point, the girls performed a rap song they'd written:

> *It's 30 years and we're going strong*
> *We thought we would put this down in song*
> *We've got a staff that can't be beat*
> *And a boss who's chic and really neat*
> *Our students can really drive us nuts*
> *But we don't take any ifs, ands, or buts,*
> *From first at Charles to then St. Clair*
> *Now we've landed at Trinity Square*
> *In another 30 years we'll still be there*
> *Moving and grooving under geriatric care!*

Before "J" was to start the job, I invited him to a pre-New Years party I'd planned for the staff. This was an annual event. We'd serve hors d'ouevres and drinks and wish one another a Happy New Year. I thought this would be a good chance for J to meet the entire staff.

"Great," he said, "I'll be in Toronto anyway that day so I'll be there."

He arrived at the party and almost immediately approached one of my teachers, Jill Duggan. He reached into his pocket and brought out a sprig of mistletoe and held it over her head and proceeded to plant his lips on hers and gave her a French kiss! Jill couldn't believe this man she'd just met was so aggressive and downright rude. She came over to me as J made his way to the next staff member.

"Who is that jerk?!" Jill asked.

I said, "Believe it or not, that's our new sales manager. Or shall I say, he was going to be our new sales manager."

I took him aside and told him his behaviour was unprofessional, insulting and totally unacceptable and this arrangement was not going to work out. Goodbye.

Occasionally, people disappointed me — like E, a permanent employee in charge of PR. Behind my back, she and another girl took our graduating students and did photo shoots with them. If she'd just come to me and said, "Eleanor, I have an idea. What I'd like to do is set up a specialty studio just doing photo shoots for the models," I might have considered a partnership. But it was the way it was done. I had to find out about it third-hand. It hurts when you trust someone and they disappoint you, especially when you consider them a friend.

Then there was the night I went out with two of our counsellors, one longtime male employee and one new counsellor, M. After we finished our dinner, I left the waiter enough cash to pay for our dinners, plus a tip. As we got up and were heading out the door, the waiter came running after us saying we hadn't paid for our meal. Someone had obviously scooped up the money and pocketed it. It was very strange. (Never leave cash on the table.)

A little while later, I figured out that it must have been M, because there were more incidents of disappearing money. I fired her, telling her never to set foot inside our office again or I'd report her to the police.

Shortly after, I got a call from Judy Welch, one of my former models, who now owned her own modelling agency in Toronto. M had gone straight over to her looking for a similar job. M figured because we were competitors Judy probably wouldn't phone me. She'd given Judy a big long story about how she worked for me but she'd heard that Judy was the best so she left me. Judy bought it and hired her. Not only that, she gave her a place to stay at her house! One night I got a call from Judy. "I'm so mad at you!"

"Why?" I asked.

"Because I hired M!" Apparently M had walked off with Judy's silverware, money, jewelry, you name it, and had disappeared.

"Oh Judy, I'm sorry. Why didn't you call me? I would have told you all about her."

What a lesson. M was a top-notch con artist and we both fell for it. The police never did locate her.

Models sometimes let me down, too. I would spend a lot of time and effort helping them to achieve their potential, then suddenly they'd just leave — no explanation, nothing. No mention of where they were going or why. It could be a vicious, cut-throat business. The minute a model achieved a certain level of success, there were 25 agents coming out of the woodwork pursuing her, promising her the moon. "You're going to make double what you're earning now." It was hard for the models because they hadn't been out in the real world long enough and they'd be wooed, and sometimes they'd leave. Then they'd be so disappointed because it wasn't the same. They'd come back and say, "Eleanor, I was a just a number out there. Here I was a person and I felt wanted and needed." The ones that were gracious enough to be honest and tell me they wanted to try something else always knew the door was open for them if they changed their minds, and often they did come back.

Some of them didn't have the decency to come and see me personally and talk to me. I don't understand people who don't have the good manners to talk face-to-face but rather just skulk away. That's the worst possible thing they can do. I don't care if they're scared or nervous. Everyone's anxious in certain situations. You deal with the discomfort and do the right thing, especially if someone has always treated you well. Otherwise you will always regret your cowardly actions.

David Niven, in his book *The Moon's a Balloon*, talks about leaving the agent he'd had for 30 years because another agent promised him the moon. He said it was the worst thing he'd ever done in his life and he never recovered from it, because he'd lost his closest friend. He'd betrayed him for pie in the sky. So even a huge star like David Niven was susceptible to an enticing sales pitch.

On the Move — St. Clair Avenue West

Again we needed larger premises, so in 1985 we listed with our realtor friend Tony Amodeo (God bless him). He felt certain he had found the perfect place and would not relent until I went with him to see a certain building on St. Clair Avenue West.

I told him, "Tony, I don't want to see it. It's in the West End, and I'm not a west ender. It has to be central." Finally, just to shut him up, I agreed to look at it.

The minute I walked in, I started laughing, because it was so perfect. It was like it had been designed for us. It was a beautiful, two-storey, freestanding building. I did have to think about the location, but the streetcar stop was right in front, and I just fell in love with the building. I made the decision the same day.

"Oh Tony," I said, "you're too much. Thank you!"

He said, "I knew it was right for you, if I could only get you out here."

And that's how we came to buy 791 St. Clair Avenue West. I

needed the main floor and basement and wanted to rent out the second floor. The previous owners had renovated the main floor and basement but not the second floor. My husband, Bruno, saw the space and said, "You know you'll never rent the second floor unless you renovate it entirely." What, more expenses! But of course I had to listen to him. So Bruno redesigned it and renovated — and he was right. We rented it instantly to Skills for Change, a non-profit organization half-owned by the government that provided immigrant employment services. They were the perfect tenants. That helped immensely with our debt load.

Just as I had no idea about construction and architecture, Bruno had little interest in my business, although he was very supportive. Looking back, I realize that without the help and expertise of my husband, my business never could have grown so fast. What he did so easily and quickly would have taken me years. Thank you, my love.

We opened 791 St. Clair Avenue West on July 6, 1984. It was a huge success from day one. Everyone loved the new facilities.

In 1985, we opened our new location at 791 St. Clair Avenue West.

Showing New York What Canadians Are Made Of

I joined the Modeling Association of America (MAA) around 1968 — one of only two Canadians, the other being Audrey Morris from Montreal, whom I knew and admired.

The enrollment at my school at that time was around 2000 students and the agency was growing, around 300 or more registered models and actors. I was doing really well, and I joined the Modeling Association of America to reach a broader, more international market. Many of the top American and European schools and agencies were members. At the time I was probably a little intimidated by New York — the centre of the fashion industry — and I figured I could observe and learn.

The MAA had an annual weeklong convention in New York. All the schools and agencies brought up-and-coming models to be showcased, mostly through runway exposure. Various international agents were invited and would observe and choose those models they

At the MAA Convention at the Waldorf Astoria, New York, 1974. I'm second from right.

might like to book for print or fashion. In those days, if you had an agency you had a school and if you had a school you had an agency. That's changed now — there are more agencies than schools — but back then you had to be trained before you went into modelling.

In my first year attending the MAA convention, my impressions totally changed. The MAA had a lot of members with schools and agencies in several U.S. states, and every one of them thought they were the biggest and the best. They had no reticence whatever in tooting their own horns. It was obvious to me that they thought we were just ham-and-eggers from Canada. What I observed within a short period of time was that some of them didn't know much about our industry. We were, as members, all assigned certain showcases to present to the agents. Some of these shows they presented were terribly amateurish. That first year, I sat back and observed the many fashion shows and workshops. I thought, I can do better than what I'm seeing. I *do* do better than what I'm seeing.

Out of all the schools and agencies in attendance, there were about five that I considered at the same level at which I pegged myself. I quickly got to know the owners and we became friends. We'd share ideas over drinks or coffee and talk about our schools and agencies, because we could help each other — we weren't competing within the same cities. We were all anxious to improve and willingly shared our knowledge with one another, which was extremely helpful both at the convention and throughout the year.

The second year brought me a very interesting experience. Toward the end of the week of the convention — they saved the best for last — there was the Professional Models Fashion Show, the big fashion show where your best model talent would be entered to be seen by all the top agents from New York, Paris, London, etc. The convention was at the Waldorf Astoria, and I was there with Traute Siebert, my school manager, teacher and Dynasty model. I also took some of our new models, whom we entered in the Junior Division fashion show earlier in the week. When you're in New York, you must go to the theatre, so Traute and I decided that on the night of the Professional Models Show, as we were not involved, we were going to take a night off and see a New York play. We were on the elevator heading out to dinner and the theatre, when I said, "Let's just peek in at the professional show and see what's happening before we go to the theatre." She agreed. We'd just take a quick peek and be on our way.

Well, the elevator door opened and we could hardly step out. It was utter chaos. The models were frantically shoving and yelling. I thought, What is going on here? We worked our way through the crowd of models to the man who was in charge and said, "Why are all these models here? They're supposed to be backstage. Aren't they doing the show?"

This poor man was having a heart attack. "The lady who was supposed to coordinate and run the show hasn't shown up. We can't find her anywhere!" Turned out the woman who was supposedly handling the show was intimidated by the 400 or so model hopefuls waiting for instruction and the top agents waiting for the show and she just took off — just packed her bags and went home without a word to anyone. She probably walked in, took a look around, and thought, No, can't do it.

These models had come from all over the world for the opportunity to be seen by top agents and at great expense. This was the most important night of their lives! I said, "There are about 20 top international agents waiting to see these young hopefuls, and you don't have a show? What is your back-up plan?"

"I don't have one! Eleanor, please help me!"

I grabbed Traute. "You and I are going to do this show, okay? We're not going to the theatre." What choice was there? You had

400 models waiting to be seen, having paid their money to come to New York. What are you going to say: "Gee, sorry"? It was incomprehensible to me.

I said to Traute, who has marvelous organizational skills, "Take them all backstage, sort them into juniors, women, men, children, mature — five divisions." So she quickly went backstage and yelled, "You, over there! You, right here! What do you mean, you have to go! There's no time to go. Stay right there until you're called."

Now that Traute was fully in charge backstage, I went out to deal with the agents, who were becoming very agitated, not knowing what was going on. No one had told them anything yet. I went up on stage and took the mic. "Hello everybody. I'm Eleanor Fulcher from Toronto, Canada, and I'm coordinating this show." I explained that there'd been a slight problem but everything was fine now. What would they like to drink? I calmed them down, got them some champagne, and assured them the show would start in a few minutes.

I had no idea what came next. I was winging it, but I knew that every one of these models was going to be seen. I told everyone backstage to come out and tell me their name and where they were from. I would then announce them. So we started with the Juniors, about 75 of them. "And now we have so and so from San Diego, California." Somehow we got through it. Every single agent stayed till the end and it went past 1 a.m.

What a night that was. I remember some of the agents saying, "Thank you. What's your name again? Where are you from?" They seemed very satisfied. I'm sure a lot of modelling careers were launched that evening.

The next year they asked me to organize the Junior Models Showcase, which I agreed to do. It was a great success. I wasn't content with the models just walking the runway one at a time and turning around and walking back like robots; that was very boring to me. I choreographed the whole thing. People were shocked. "Eleanor, when did you choreograph this?"

I said, "At 2 a.m. It was the only time the ballroom was available. This is showbiz. They didn't come all the way to New York to sleep; they were happy to be in the ballroom at 2 a.m. to rehearse."

I remember prior to the show, the president of the MAA at that time, knowing I was Canadian, still had some doubts about my ability. I'm sure they all thought Canada was a cultural desert and that Canadians wore muklucks and lived in igloos. She came up to me before the show and said, "Okay Eleanor, here's what we're going to do. I'll introduce you and ...blah, blah, blah."

I said, "Wait a minute. I'll tell you what we're going to do. This is my show. You told me to do it, now you go sit in the audience and enjoy it. I will introduce you. You stand up and take a bow. You are the president but you are not in charge of this segment. So just relax and enjoy the show."

She didn't know what to do with this arrogant person from Canada; she just stood there looking at me trying to figure out whether to believe all this. "You're sure, Eleanor?"

"I'm positive. It's okay. Just go and sit and relax."

The show got a standing ovation. Immediately after that show I was asked if I would accept the role of president of the MAA. The Modeling Association of America was a volunteer organization. I had my hands full keeping up with my own business, so I agreed to accept the office of vice president, not president. During this term, it was obvious to me that MAA needed a permanent coordinator. A salaried position. It would take a person one year full-time to do what we were trying to do pro bono in our spare (spare?) time. We'd have all these conference calls and I'd be trying to get hold of an agent in Utah and someone else in Florida — I didn't have time for that. I told them there was a huge opportunity for someone to start a new organization for profit, and sure enough the next year one of our "group of five" from Texas started the International Modeling Association of America. It eventually outgrew MAA due to the total dedication of one person.

The MAA had been responsible for setting standards within the industry, and one incident brought home to me that we needed to have some guidance on ethics. Part of our school curriculum was teaching social graces and etiquette, but one day, when I had put the "Reserved" sign on a table at an MAA luncheon, an MAA member had taken my sign off and put her own sign on the table. I confronted her and said, "Excuse me, this table is reserved," and she just turned away. This is the way some of them were. So when I was vice president, I told them we needed some guidelines — that we needed to respect each other and treat each other as we'd like to be treated. If we were teaching social graces and etiquette in our curriculum, let's practise what we preach.

The American attitude toward Canadians then was, "Oh…you're from Canada." Like we were second-class citizens. They knew nothing about Canada. So it was really important to me to make "Canadian" synonymous with excellence.

The MAA wanting me to be president was groundbreaking. A Canadian? I like to think that in some small way this development had something to do with changing their attitude and their image of Canadians — and Canadian models.

Over the years, I became the spokesperson for Canadian models. They were and are world class and deserve equal recognition. At every opportunity, I made that clear to anyone who'd listen. I was once asked to be a guest speaker at the Granite Club in Toronto, defending Canadian models. Many top Canadian models were there and they all loved what I had to say about Canadian models being able to compete with the best in the world. Time has shown how right I was.

But there was this attitude in the '60s that of course New York models are better than Canadian models. In an article in *Liberty* magazine, Canadians like Ken Bell, a fashion photographer, were quoted as saying, "Canadian models talk too much and don't concentrate on their jobs." And Paul Harriett, a TV producer, saying, "Canadian models should be more aggressive, need more personality." Chris Bruhn, a fashion stylist with a top catalogue house, said, "New York models move well and work quicker than Canadian girls." What? Unbelievable! Rubbish!

Whenever I had the chance, I promoted the huge potential of Canadian models. This was an article in *Liberty* magazine about the search for a Canadian fashion model. The winner of the contest won an Eleanor Fulcher modelling course and a modelling contract.

Lower left, I welcome the winner, Patricia Ann Falvey, to Toronto. Centre, she and I sign her contract. Right, my friend and makeup artist George Abbott.

It was an interesting period in my life because it gave me so much more confidence about what we had here in Canada. At the time, the Canadian modelling field was inundated with American models and agencies, like the Ford Agency. Our top Canadian clients would always go to New York to hire American models; there was very little support for our Canadian models. Large companies that produced fashion catalogues, like Eaton's and Simpson's, would send reps down to New York to hire American models and fly the models to Toronto and pay them top photography rates while taking jobs away from Canadian models. Eventually, some of us intervened and complained to the government; that's how serious it was. Finally, the government passed a law saying that no American models could get work permits if the clients had not auditioned Canadian models first. If these rules were not followed we had a phone number to call to complain. At last!

The Ford agency was the number one agency in the world, run by Eileen and Jerry Ford. I decided this would be a good contact for our agency. Eileen Ford only worked with agents she selected, and that didn't include me. So I thought, Fine, I'll go to New York to her place of business and make a pitch for our agency. It was important for me to get my foot in the door. I'll never forget that meeting.

Eileen's husband, Jerry, was there — such a charmer and a real gentleman. He invited me in and we chatted for a while. I really liked him and we hit it off. I'd finished showing him the pictures of the models when the receptionist buzzed and said that Eileen was going to join the meeting.

In she walks, right over to the window, doesn't shake hands with me or acknowledge me in any way, turns her back on me. It's just beyond imagination, the rudeness. She told me she dealt with Betty Milne in Toronto and I said, "I'm aware of that, and I'm not expecting you to *not* deal with Betty. I just thought you might want to leave the door open to deal with us, too." She flipped through our head sheets without comment and left. I could see Jerry was embarrassed at her behaviour.

When I left, I was outside hailing a cab when she came flying out, pushed me aside, and jumped in my cab, saying, "You can walk to your hotel — it's just three blocks," and was gone. Welcome to New York.

If she was that unpleasant to me, I'm sure she was to others, as well. I wasn't surprised therefore when one of Ford's top models, Wilhelmina, opened her own New York agency and models flooded to work with her. No wonder. She was not only the world's top model but also absolutely charming. We became friends and business associates. Wilhelmina came to Toronto once with her husband, Bruce Cooper. Bruno and I took them to dinner. We went to Julie's, one of the best restaurants in Toronto back then, and had a wonderful time. Bruce seemed fascinated by Bruno's architectural business. Bruno had talked about this building he had just finished and how there

Bruno and I enjoying dinner with internationally famous model Wilhelmina and her husband, Bruce Cooper. From *Toronto Life*, 1971

was a model of it on the roof of his office building — it was too big to keep in the office — and both Bruce and Wilhelmina really wanted to see it. So after dinner, the four of us climbed up the fire escape, in the dark, onto the roof of this building so we could see the building model — and it was raining!

As I mentioned, Bruno was never really involved in my business, other than when I needed space for expansion, because he was totally involved in international real estate development and travelled a great deal, especially to Europe. I suspect that Bruce, who was a former producer for Johnny Carson's *Tonight* show, also had many other business interests outside of Wilhelmina's agency, but gave it all up when they married to help her launch her new agency.

Wilhelmina enjoyed our evening together immensely and chatted with Bruno in German occasionally (Bruno is Swiss German and Wilhelmina is German). We at last had a great agency contact in New York — and two good friends.

CHAPTER 4

ELEANOR FULCHER SPA — THE FIRST SPA IN CANADA

I fell in love — head over heels in love — with a cottage in Muskoka. The affair started quite innocently. I had wanted to rent a nice cottage for the summers so Bruno and I could escape whenever possible with our two children, Angela and Marcus, and our nanny. I was working hard and thought that during July and August I could have meetings in Toronto for Tuesday and Thursday, driving back and forth, and spend the rest of the week working from the cottage and hanging out with the kids.

I had put an ad in the paper and had three places in Muskoka to look at, none of which I liked after checking them out. On my way back to Toronto I thought I may as well drop in to see this fourth place. I hadn't really considered it, as I thought it was way too big and not what I was looking for at all, but it was on my way back so I thought, What the heck. I drove down Highway 169 to Shady

Lane, turned left and went down a small incline. And there was the view. That was it. I fell in love. It's like our house on Castle Frank Road — something has to touch you, and that setting touched me. The cottage was right on the water, with a beautiful panoramic view. I thought, This is how I imagined it to be in Muskoka — God's tranquilizer. (I read that somewhere.)

The cottage belonged to a man who had won the property on a gambling debt! He owned another cottage, and he couldn't have cared less about this place. It had a main house plus four separate suites (which we didn't need). It was huge and needed attention. We rented it for two summers. Angela was seven and Marcus was five when we started going up there in 1975. We went every weekend and everyone loved it, and in 1977 my company bought it.

The main reason I wanted to buy it was that I had an idea that I'd like to open a spa. I'd been to one in Switzerland and thought it was absolute heaven, being pampered, having a massage and a swim and a facial. Spas were common in Europe but I didn't know of any in Canada. I thought that was a shame, because I sure needed that pampering sometimes and I was sure other businesswomen did too. Then the idea came to me — the property would make a perfect spa! Imagine the number of businesswomen that needed to get away for a week and just unwind! The next thing I knew we were making plans for the first spa in Canada. The Muskoka setting was perfect and Bruno was up for the challenge. (Never say to an architect, "I wonder what we could do with this…?")

The man who had lost this cottage through a gambling debt was a dentist who had lived there and ran his dental practice from there. He was also a would-be handyman who had attempted to renovate and enlarge the building, but when Bruno examined the structure carefully, he said the beams were in danger of falling down because they weren't reinforced properly. The contractor we hired said it was

The Eleanor Fulcher Spa on Lake Muskoka, Ontario

The Spa, "Before."

Spa brochure

With extensive renovations, we created a warm, relaxing environment

built with matchsticks — that one good storm and it would cave in. We were told that there was no way it would have passed the building code regulations. We suspected there had been a "contra" deal involved — teeth for a permit. (Sound familiar?) We had to rebuild the entire cottage. Thank goodness Bruno was there to supervise the trades. They weren't used to people being so fussy. They'd finish their specific area and Bruno would arrive on the weekend, take a look and say, "The beam (or whatever) doesn't go all the way to the end there. It's half an inch off." And they had to do the whole thing again. They soon realized he meant business so they started to apply their best skills. To this day, they use the spa as representative of their finest project because they're so proud of it. It was ultimately perfect and will no doubt stand the test of time.

Throughout the renovations, even the indoor pool had to be dug up because the measurements were uneven and they couldn't lay the tiles properly. They had to re-excavate the entire pool and start from scratch. Then the local health inspector got on the case and dissected every little thing; I think he was making up the regulations as he went along, as they had no idea what a spa was. We had to take the diving board down because the pool wasn't deep enough. (It had been there for years.) We had to change all the toilet lids so they'd be more "sanitary" for women. Create all sorts of signs. And on and on. All this cost lots and lots of money. Everything we were earning in the city was going into this undertaking. I thought I would go broke or insane — or both.

When I finally ran out of money, I decided I needed to sell 50 percent of the building at 791 St. Clair Avenue West to raise more funds. A longtime friend of ours in Berlin, Dr. Wolfgang Feil, a wealthy banker, came to mind, because over the years he had told me he admired my business acumen and if I ever needed an investment partner... He was true to his word. One phone call and he

My dear friend
Dr. Wolfgang Feil
and me.

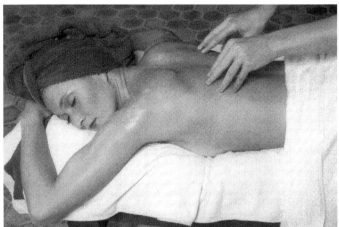

Guests at the Spa could practise yoga and enjoy a massage,
neither of which was common back then.

wired the money in two hours. I couldn't believe it. He came along just at the right time, because by that time I was desperate. For $350,000 he became co-owner of my building at 791 St. Clair Avenue West and I was able to get out of debt and finish the spa project. Thank you, Wolfgang, for believing in my dream — and in me. You are a true friend — and a lifesaver!

It took three years of renovating before the Eleanor Fulcher Spa opened in 1980 — it was a huge undertaking. Obviously, if I'd known what it was going to entail I'd never have started. We had to go through the whole re-zoning mess at Gravenhurst city hall to open it as a spa (heavy lawyer fees involved in that process). The town should have been thanking us because now there was a beautiful property where before there'd been an eyesore. Clients would be coming to Muskoka and spending money. But the locals were uneasy because they had their own ideas of what a spa was. In our ads, we listed all the services — diet, fitness, facials, reflexology, massage, aquafit. One night Bruno and I were out for dinner in Gravenhurst and overheard two men saying, "Well, they're giving 'massages.' You know what that means." Oh, good grief!

Action was needed to quell these ridiculous rumours. So I invited the mayor and his committee to a cocktail party at the Spa to explain the concept and give them a tour. I then invited all their wives for a full day at the Spa where they enjoyed the many activities and dining. Once they understood the concept, they were 100 percent behind it. I got wonderful local press.

Even the famous *Segwun* cruise steamship changed its route to pass by the Spa. Bruno and I had the opportunity to meet the captain while having lunch on the *Segwun* when the Spa had just opened. I said, "What a shame the *Segwun* couldn't pass closer to us." The captain pondered for a moment and invited us into his quarters, pulled out huge navigational maps and studied them. He pointed out

The Segwun steamship cruised past the Spa

to us that there was a narrow passage of water separating Rankin Island from the mainland. In checking depth levels he noted that if the *Segwun* went straight down the middle, there was sufficient depth at that point to allow the *Segwun* to pass right by the Spa — which he did for the next ten years, and every time he announced, "And there is the Eleanor Fulcher Spa, the first spa in Canada." Toot, toot, toot, and we all waved. Hallelujah!

There was only room for 12 guests each week, which was perfect. I developed a regular clientele of mostly businesswomen who'd come up every year to lose five or so pounds and enjoy the many services — sometimes the same five or so pounds they'd lost the previous year at the Spa! They made the Spa week their vacation and they looked forward to it. On each Friday night I would drive up and they'd put on a little show for me while I took lots of pictures — great fun. What great women — bright, funny and sharp.

Ours was a friendly Spa and everyone knew everyone else by name. It was not only about losing weight and exercising. It was a

Fulcher's spa is incredible

The first thing that greets anyone entering the Eleanor Fulcher Spa on the outskirts of Gravenhurst is the peaceful ambience. Lush greenery is everywhere, and the decor of country elegance is captured in the warmest earth tones.

The workmanship is impeccable, from the brick fireplace to the inlaid Italian tile floor. The soothing classical music which met me upon my arrival only further enticed me to enter.

From furnishings to upholstery, every aspect of this place is carefully and tastefully presented, and touches such as an arched brick doorway and a gorgeous wooden dining room ceiling indicate the attention to detail that went into the structure. All is delightfully enhanced by the spectacular view of Lake Muskoka and the bright sun beaming through the countless picture windows. It is quite a place, and Eleanor Fulcher can certainly be applauded for the flawless work inside.

But alas, it wasn't always the elegant retreat it is today. It is the product of five years of painstaking work, a seemingly endless project which met one difficulty after another. Due to the poor workmanship of the existing site, nearly the entire structure had to be totally reconstructed, all done under the careful eye of Ms. Fulcher's architect husband. It is impossible to even imagine that so many problems arose, because now all that remains is beauty. I'm glad they held so firmly to their idea and saw it through; and so are the many satisfied guests who have already enjoyed the benefits of this health spa.

Popular particularly in Europe and the U.S., spas such as this are becoming more and more integral part of the modern woman's lifestyle. Spas offer one an opportunity to take some time off a busy schedule and devote that time to the cleansing and relaxation of body and mind, engaging in a carefully planned regime of exercise, diet, and skin care which will hopefully be continued in the participant's daily life.

Here you can count on definite results. Weight reduction, inch loss, internal cleansing, and effective skin treatments are but a few of the benefits of spa programmes. And a setting such as this one in the midst of the country is indeed a peaceful getaway for any city dweller. One returns home refreshed, renewed, and armed with a personal fitness programme and specific routines of skin care and diet necessary for a post spa follow-up.

Women who have attended spas all over the world have remarked that nowhere else have they been given such individual attention, for here the attendance is limited to 10 guests per week.

The cosy rooms offer twin beds, bath, and a glorious lake view, each one decorated in bright country prints. Among the facilities are a whirlpool, massage room, swimming pool, sauna, games room, etc. The dining room features the most spectacular view of all, as it overlooks the lake. This room is met with a rustic brick fireplace on one side, and a handsome bar on the other where attendants enjoy their happy hour and a choice of refreshing blends of either juice beverages or wine cocktails.

A day at the spa would consist of such activities as a morning jog, exercises, dance exercise, aquabic, and evening yoga. There are several "free time" periods at which time the guests can partake of a massage, sauna, whirlpool, an herb facial, or aroma therapy.

Other activities of the day are a discussion group in which the ladies discuss a wide range of topics of their choosing, such as business, etiquette, or lifestyles; and evening movies on the spa's home video set. All are usually eager to enjoy a good night's rest after their nightly herbal tea.

The menu offers a nutritionally balanced 800 calorie diet of protein, fresh fruits and vegetables, all deliciously presented by the cheerful chef. The spa has an excellent staff, all ready to assist you in your programme.

But truly, the success of the spa is due to Eleanor Fulcher herself. She is the evidence of what her spa plan hopes to offer all who engage it: a way of life in which the demands of a successful career, a family life, and a sensible beauty regime can be effectively dovetailed.

As she states on the spa's brochure: "That's why after 20 years of running my own beauty business I decided to open a spa — a spa dedicated to women who acknowledge that fitness is a must, but need a professional push in the right direction."

A great review from the *Gravenhurst News*

place to relax, connect with other women, and ground yourself. Some women just wanted to lie out on the dock instead of taking part in every activity, and that was just fine. I organized group discussions where the women would spend an hour or so in this cozy sitting area near the fireplace, just talking and sharing stories and experiences. It became one of the highlights of the day. It was therapeutic and promoted camaraderie. Much later, when other spas appeared on the scene, some of our clients told me that at other spas it was impersonal, whereas at ours there was a wonderful, friendly, helpful atmosphere. Exactly what I'd envisioned.

We had four hours of fitness a day, consisting of time in the pool, walks in the morning, and fitness, yoga and dance classes. The nutritionist put clients who wanted to lose weight on a diet of 800 calories a day and warned them at the beginning they were going to rebel. They'd hate everyone, including me. I told them they could lie

The ideal fitness vacation!

THE ELEANOR FULCHER SPA ON BEAUTIFUL LAKE MUSKOKA IS FOR WOMEN OF ALL AGES WHO WANT TO SHAPE-UP AND FEEL WONDERFUL. LOSE 5lbs. AND UP TO 10ins. IN JUST ONE WEEK!

THE SPA PLAN INCLUDES: DELECTABLE LOW CALORIE MEALS, FACIAL, MASSAGE, SAUNA, AROMATHERAPY, YOGA, AEROBICS, DANCERSIZE, WHIRLPOOL, DISCUSSION GROUPS, MOVIES, AND RETURN TRANSPORTATION FROM THE ROYAL YORK HOTEL.

ISN'T IT TIME YOU PAMPERED YOURSELF?

A personalized spa for all seasons limited to 10 pampered guests per week

The Eleanor Fulcher Spa

For reservation or brochure call

416-653-9110

One of my Spa ads

down or skip some of the fitness if they were tired but that if they stuck to it they would get the results they wanted.

The goal was to lose five or more pounds in the seven days. The first four or five pounds drop off really fast when you're in a program like this, and if you lose more, that's incredible. But it's the inches that start to come off even within the week; it's amazing. The weight loss slows down when they leave but that first week they need that incentive to carry on once they returned home. At the end of the week was the payoff — weight loss and inches off, with a small prize for whoever lost the most.

Some of the clients would occasionally cheat on their diet and drive into town and buy a chocolate bar. Once the housekeeper came to me with a chocolate bar wrapper and said, "I found this in the garbage in Unit 2." So after that I hired a bus and clients were picked up at the Royal York Hotel in Toronto and returned there a week later. This way, they couldn't drive into town — and thus avoided temptation!

The business was constantly evolving. I'd listen to what my clients told me and sometimes adjust the program accordingly. I did everything I could to make it a great week for them. For instance, an important time for some of these women was their cocktail at the end of the day, so the nutritionist created a special drink for Happy Hour. Except instead of alcohol we'd serve Blushing Bunnies — tomato juice and buttermilk. They'd sit at the bar (yes, we had a bar) and have these delicious low-calorie drinks in stem glasses. It seemed to satisfy the urge to have a drink. Another time someone mentioned she wished we offered pedicures, so that very week I went out and bought the equipment. I hired my next-door neighbour, Bobbi, who used to do professional manicures and pedicures in Hungary. She was perfect. She loved her job at the Spa and never stopped thanking me — and she lived next door. How lucky was that?

The Eleanor Fulcher Spa operated from 1980 to 1990. It was a

A typical photo op. Don't try it!

seasonal business from May to October — winters are rough in Muskoka — so I had to make the most of the months when it was open.

Since spas were still almost totally unknown in Canada I had to work diligently at getting the attention of the media. One day I got a call from CTV. "We've heard good things about your Spa and we'd like to interview you and your staff in a week or so — maybe about 15 minutes of TV time." I was thrilled. A full interview on CTV? Absolute gold. CTV would be bringing their entire crew! I was excited and immediately started preparations.

The crew was coming up Monday. Only one week to prepare and we had a full house of clients. Then things started to fall apart. The pool maintenance man, who always came twice a day to check chlorine levels, etc., was told by my Spa manager that he didn't need to come in — that I had made other arrangements! Which was simply not true. Thus, no pool maintenance all week. Of course that wreaked havoc on the bacteria count, resulting in several women getting ear infections.

On Friday I got a call from the Gravenhurst health inspector telling me they had closed the Spa for "health" reasons — bacteria in the pool. He also phoned CTV and advised them to cancel the shoot. I found this out on Friday night. The CTV crew was booked for Monday. Bruno and I were going out for dinner with some friends and all through dinner I was so mad I could hardly see straight! Sometimes you need to get mad to get going, and I got going.

I apologized for cutting dinner short and went home. I got on the phone to find this health inspector because he was the only person who could reopen the Spa. It just so happened that this was a Friday night of a long weekend and all businesses were closed. I finally got a phone number (after checking out four other surnames) and a young girl answered. I asked if her daddy was there and she said he didn't live there any more (divorced). After a nice chat with her she gave me the phone number of where he lived.

After I finally reached him and identified myself, he said in disbelief, "How did you ever find me?" I told him it was a long story but I needed to see him immediately (I may have threatened to sue the township) to straighten out this problem and allow CTV to film. He agreed to see me the next day.

So Bruno and my new Spa director (gorgeous and widowed four years) met with him. We explained the problem. He then called my pool maintenance man, who confirmed the story. Fortunately, I always worked with local trades and they all knew one another. The health inspector called CTV to assure them that the Spa was fine and that our pool maintenance man would empty and refill the pool over the weekend. They agreed to go ahead with the story. I also had to call all the clients who had ear infections, because they could have sued me. I explained that what had happened was foul play and they were all shocked and sympathetic and glad that I had personally called them. They all accepted my offer of either a free week at the Spa or their money back, and signed a waiver. Disaster averted.

Monday morning came and the CTV crew arrived. I had brought up ten of my models and staff to stand in for clients and had everything lined up. I was running around coordinating each and every segment — about six hours of footage. The CTV coordinator thought it would be nice to end the story by interviewing me sitting by the fireplace in the pool room — a nice, friendly relaxed final shoot. So I lit the fire and ran off to do my makeup. But when I got back to the pool room, it was filled with smoke. You couldn't see a thing. I had forgotten to open the fireplace flue.

At this point I didn't know whether to laugh or cry. I told everyone to help themselves to drinks, opened the flue, cleared the smoke out, and after about an hour, we did sit down and do the interview.

After they left, I couldn't believe I got through it, but as I watched them all leave, quite happy with the footage, I remember thinking, I did it! It was one of those days in my life that I will never, ever forget.

It was sabotage, perpetrated by my Spa director who had worked for me for seven years. She had given me her notice and was leaving at the end of the week to travel in the U.S., so naturally I didn't think of featuring her in the show, as she would have been gone when the story ran. She must have decided that if she couldn't do the TV show, then no one would! Oh dear. If she had just come to me and said, "Eleanor, I'm hurt that you aren't going to allow me to be part of the television show," we could have talked about it and probably could have worked it out. All that distress, anger, and near disaster — it could have been avoided with a frank and open discussion. I could have sued her but strangely, I felt sorry for her. Years later, at a social gathering, she begged me to forgive her. Which I did. Life's too short to carry a grudge.

Anyway, we got through the day. The TV special ran shortly after and was a fantastic boost for the Spa. The calls came flooding in. Never give up!

A very reliable source told me that many top chefs are alcoholics, and the glass of water they have beside them when preparing meals is actually vodka. I can understand that. Just preparing dinner for eight requires a drink or two to calm me, never mind 40 or 400! I had a few experiences with chefs at the Spa. One in particular stands out in my mind. I had invited my friend Joan Frankel up to give me her input as a guest, and after dinner one evening she came to me in the pool room and whispered, "Eleanor, I think you should come with me to the kitchen — *now*." I followed her quickly and to my utter amazement the kitchen floor was covered foot-high with soapsuds! We have a small washer and dryer hidden in a kitchen cupboard for the chef's use — it's very handy for tea towels and aprons and so on. The chef was nowhere to be found. Apparently, she was last seen jumping off the diving board (fully clothed). When I found her, she was passed out across her bed. In her hurry to get to the pool (and sober up?) she had dumped a full box of Tide into the washer, and the suds had seeped out little by little until they covered the entire kitchen. The plumber had to replace the washer, as he was unable to flush it out.

The Spa, as such, was a success. But as a business endeavour, it was not, because it couldn't turn a profit. I would have had to double the rates or add four more suites, with the same number of staff. Bruno told me the zoning bylaws didn't allow any expansion.

In 1989 the King Ranch Spa opened in King City. I was invited to their opening and I could not believe my eyes how lavish it was. The money they invested was incredible — I heard it was about $30 million. Even the staff had their own rooms and annual employment contracts. (My employees usually had contracts for three or four months only.) Was I missing something? I was happy someone else was entering the spa field — competition can be healthy for all — but somewhat skeptical of their approach. Year round? Winter in Ontario?

My clients told me they were curious to try King Ranch. So I decided to close my Spa that year and encouraged my clients to visit King Ranch for comparison. The rate was the same — they offered a 50 percent discount to first-time clients. I rented my Spa for the entire season to a large corporation who wanted it as a training facility for their employees. They didn't require any of my staff — no nutritionist, no fitness director, no cook, no masseuse. Just a housekeeper. I quoted them the usual rate for twelve guests and they said that's fine and we'll take it for the whole summer. No arguments, no negotiating. This was amazing. And I actually ended up with a profit! So after that eye-opening season I decided to reinvent the Spa and rent it out corporately. No headaches, no worries — and a profit to boot!

Today there are hundreds of spas in Canada and I'm sure their task of starting up was made easier thanks to the Eleanor Fulcher Spa. At least now, "spas" have their own listing in the Yellow Pages, not under Recreational Facilities, which I had to fight to change. But most spas today are not booked by the week, but rather by treatment or by the hour or day. It was certainly a challenge.

Incidentally, King Ranch closed in 1992 when the bank repossessed the facility. I had offered all my ten years of spa experience and advice to their manager months before they opened — but no one was listening.

CHAPTER 5

TRIALS AND TRIBULATIONS

One thing I've learned in life is that if you're right, you fight — even if it becomes a court battle. Do not give in; do not cave to intimidation. I learned that lesson so many times when I was in business. Sometimes it's just a matter of principle. Over the years, I came to the conclusion that if you own a business, sooner or later you're going to get sued. I had a policy in the school and agency — that I personally would handle everything of a legal nature. I knew how upsetting it was the first couple of times I had to go through our legal system. I was going to make sure none of my staff had to go through that process.

More often than not, when I represented my company, the plaintiff knew they were attempting to undermine my name and my reputation and it was very personal. They would often drop their trumped-up charges about a teacher doing this or that, or whatever it was they were trying to get money for. It led to some interesting experiences in court. I actually got quite a bit of legal experience!

Courtroom Drama

Once I had to be in court for three days fighting a ridiculous lawsuit by a man I had hired as sales manager. He was highly recommended by a professional business advisor but he turned out to be my second disaster with a male employee. I'd been advised often that men were better at sales than women and I decided to give it another try. Let me tell you something I finally learned — in my business, women are better at almost everything because they leave their egos at home. As the saying goes, Ginger Rogers could do anything Fred Astaire could do, except backwards and in high heels!

One afternoon about his third week with us, this new manager, L, poked his nose in my office and was sort of waving goodbye to me. "I'm going to the ballgame," he said. "See you in a couple of hours."

He's going to a ballgame? I hadn't been to a ballgame in years or any other afternoon event for that matter, but here's this new guy telling me he's taking off and he hasn't even been here three weeks. Plus he hadn't done anything to improve the sales department. I knew then he was not the right person. I let him go as soon as he returned from the ballgame.

Two weeks later he sued me for $100,000. He retained lawyers that work for a percentage of what they get in a settlement. I ended up in court for three days with his two lawyers. I didn't hire a lawyer, because I thought, What do I need a lawyer for? It was spelled out in the contract that either one of us could cancel the contract without notice within three months.

Now, I didn't know this at the time — I've learned a lot about the legal system — but if you don't give the plaintiff enough time to present their case fully, they can claim it was unfair — a mistrial. They can ask for a retrial. The judge has to hear them out until they present every argument, all evidence, witnesses and so on. What a waste of the court's time! Something that could have been settled in two minutes with an arbitrator was argued for three days. They were going on and on and the judge tried not to look bored listening to these guys, but at one point he said to the lawyers, "Is this going to take much longer?"

They said, "No Your Honour, about another two hours."

"Just a minute please gentlemen, just a minute." The judge turned to me. "Miss Fulcher," he said, "I'm really quite interested in your training program. I have a granddaughter, 13, very bright but she's really shy. Do you think this would be something that would be good for her?"

I said, "Oh, absolutely, Your Honour." I outlined the entire teen Butterfly program, told him the cost, and said that all teens should have the opportunity to enroll in this program in order to develop their confidence to the fullest. He listened with interest as these lawyers cooled their heels — it was such a wonderful moment!

"Thank you very much, that's really interesting Miss Fulcher. Now, gentlemen, you may continue."

So they carry on and I can see this judge is just putting in time because these lawyers aren't giving up. They questioned me about everything in my life, not at all relevant to the case. Ridiculous.

At the very end the judge asked L to take the witness stand and directed his remarks to him. "Now, I see from your resume you have a wonderful education. You've been to such-and-such university, and you have a B.A. You've won this and that award..." etc. etc., and L's sitting there all puffed up and feeling really important.

"Yes, Your Honour, yes, that's true," and so on.

Then the judge said, "Therefore, I presume you can read?"

"Uh…yes."

"Good. Now could you read this to me. Just read this paragraph in the contract, the part that is initialed here by you and Miss Fulcher. Just read that for the court please."

L read the clause aloud: "Either party may, within three months of this date, terminate this agreement without notice if not satisfied," and the contract would become null and void.

The judge said, "Now tell me, what part of that don't you understand?"

All L could do was just look at him, stunned.

"Case dismissed, costs to the plaintiff." Afterward, the judge said, "Miss Fulcher, I'm so sorry you had to go through this. But what can we do? If I cut them off, they're going to come back and say they didn't get a fair trial and it's going to be back in court again."

I was amazed. What is the point of a very explicit contract if someone can still sue you? No wonder the courts are backed up. A court-appointed arbitrator could have solved a case like this in five minutes and saved the taxpayers lots of money. But I was so impressed with the judge. He alone allowed me to believe there is still hope for our justice system.

Human Rights Commission

One day, I was informed that officials from the Ontario Human Rights Commission would be arriving at my office. They'd had a complaint against my company from a recent immigrant, an East Indian woman, who had taken our modelling program. She claimed we were prejudiced and was demanding a full refund.

I remembered this woman. I personally would give students their Final Exam Class, which was an overall assessment of their progress. If they passed they would qualify for our Model of the Year Awards Fashion Show. I'd decide if they were ready or not. If they weren't ready, they got ten or more free practice classes. So then I'd see them once or twice more, no charge, so that we could bring them up to the standards I thought each could achieve. It was a proven process that ensured a top-quality show.

At the Final Exam Class this particular student was clearly not ready and needed some more practice classes, so I told her that. She never returned. A short time later, I received this letter of complaint through the Human Rights Commission accusing me of being prejudiced and treating the woman unfairly and demanding a total refund of her money. Then the Human Rights Commission actually sent in three government employees. For three days, they interviewed my students, my staff and my teachers, in an attempt to prove this accusation.

I told my staff, "I will deal with it; you just answer their questions honestly." I wrote down everything I observed because I could not believe it. I like to think I am the least prejudiced person in business you'd ever meet. So I wasn't worried — just very annoyed.

At the end of the three days they couldn't find anything improper. In fact they saw that I employed people from many ethnic groups: East Indians, blacks, Asians. My students were also a cross-section of cultures and races.

It turned out that this woman's husband was behind it all. She confessed to me later, "Miss Fulcher, I didn't want to do it. My husband insisted that I call the government to get the money back." He wanted a refund of $800, or whatever she'd spent, and the only way he figured he'd get it was to file a complaint through the Human Rights Commission.

There was no way I was refunding her money. She had received full value and fair treatment. Finally — finally! — an appointment was set up between the accuser and me at the Human Rights office, plus the supervisor who was overseeing this absurd case. I should mention that this East Indian woman was difficult to understand. Her English was limited and this supervisor was doing his best to try to understand her problem through her broken English. I told him he had to speak very slowly for her to understand. After a while, totally exasperated, he said, "Miss Fulcher, all we need you to do is to say you're sorry to this woman."

I paused for a moment and then I agreed. I turned to her and said, "I'm sorry _____. I'm sorry that I wasn't totally honest with you. I was trying to spare your feelings. I should have told you your makeup needs lots of work, your hair needs styling, your clothes are uncoordinated, and your walk and turns are terrible. But I didn't want to hurt your feelings so I didn't come down harder on you. And for that I'm really sorry."

The supervisor didn't know where to look and finally said, "Thank you."

Case dismissed.

Fine. That episode was over, but it was far from over in my mind. I sat down and wrote letters to the prime minister, to my MPP, to my lawyer, to everyone I could think of, and explained what the government had put me through — over one complaint. I wrote, "I am a Canadian through and through, born and raised in Toronto. I'm as true a Canadian as you will ever find. I started my own business and worked hard and paid my taxes, I don't owe anyone anything, I employ a lot of people and I've tried hard all my life to be a good and honest citizen. And I get treated like this because of one complaint from one immigrant who called the Human Rights Commission. No one bothered to interview me regarding the validity of this complaint. It was just assumed that I was the guilty one. The immigrant was believed over me — she's right and I'm wrong. I ask myself, Is this the Canada I want to live in? Right now I'm ashamed of being a Canadian."

I sent the letters and got it off my chest. I didn't hear anything from the government. But three months later, I got an unusual phone call. "Eleanor," the man on the line said, "you don't know me, but I went to school with your brother, Fred. I've been following your career with interest for many years." It turned out this gentleman had been appointed the new Ontario ombudsman. I had said in my letter that what was needed was an arbitrator who would sit down and sort this kind of thing out fast instead of wasting everyone's time (not to mention our tax dollars), plus humiliating me and my staff and undermining my reputation. He said, "I thought it only right that you should know what happened as a result of your letter. It was read in Parliament." He told me he wanted me to know that my letter had a major impact. Parliament had decided to appoint an ombudsman to resolve future complaints, then send in the troops only if the ombudsman couldn't resolve the issue. As far as I know, to this day that procedure is still followed.

So don't just fume. Write a letter. Do something! If you're really upset about something, get it down in writing and send out letters. It can make a difference.

Insurance Fraud

Another time, a woman at the Spa sprained her ankle while she was out with the fitness director taking her morning walk with the other guests. But she would not go to the doctor to have it checked. I wasn't there but the Spa director reported it to me in Toronto because that was our procedure. If there was any kind of a problem, notify us, so we would have it on record.

She faxed the report to me and I phoned our insurance company and told them what had happened and that the girl was limping and was advised to go to the doctor, but she had refused. Then I sent the insurance company the written report.

End of story? No. Six months later this woman sued the Spa for $10,000, asserting we were responsible for her fractured ankle. I wasn't nervous because what could she be suing us for after all this time? Well, six months later, she'd gone to a doctor. The doctor said she had a fractured ankle. Six months after the fact. I just turned the matter over to the insurance company, knowing they had all the paperwork plus ten witnesses who knew she had refused to see a doctor. She had also been fine for the rest of her Spa week and her ankle was never mentioned again, and she participated in all the activities. I let the insurance company deal with it, knowing we had a solid case with the paperwork on file.

Time went by and I didn't hear anything more. Then one day I had to call the insurance company for something else so I asked them about it. "By the way, did anything ever happen with that Spa case I sent you?"

"Yes," they said matter-of-factly. "We settled that for $10,000." It had not been worth their while to go to court — $10,000 or less and they don't go to court!

I said, "We had a foolproof case!" I was really annoyed. That woman got an easy $10,000 and obviously knew the insurance company policies. The Spa director noted that this was this woman's second visit to the Spa and she had almost a totally different personality than the first time she'd been there. She was acting strangely and was very withdrawn. We reflected that she probably planned the whole thing.

In any event, I switched insurance companies. What kind of policy allows anyone to walk off with $10,000 — because the insurance company doesn't have time to deal with this "small" amount? Talk about encouraging this type of fraud!

Deception at Reception

In response to our ad, a girl applied for the receptionist position. Her credentials seemed quite suitable, but what struck me was she had the most incredibly sad tale. She was only 17, from out West, and her mother and father had died in a car accident. Alone, she'd decided to come to Toronto. I felt so sorry for her. I hired her as my front desk receptionist. She was also responsible for student payments and bank deposits.

After she'd been on the front desk for about six months, our cleaning man mentioned to me offhandedly, "You know, that receptionist of yours sure is keen. She's in here every Sunday."

"What do you mean, she's in here every Sunday?"

"Working. She says she's got so much work and she doesn't want to get behind."

Strange…I didn't know a thing about this. Alarm bells started to ring. I pulled out some student payment records and asked my vice-president, Joanne, to audit them. She said she'd take them home and go over them carefully. She phoned me about two hours later. "Eleanor, stop the press. We have a problem — a major problem. None of the balances are right. The books have been cooked."

I knew then what had been happening. This girl was a thief. When I asked her why she came in on Sundays, she said, "Oh, you know, I get behind. I like to feel on top of things."

A few weeks prior to this, she'd told me that she was giving notice and would be leaving the company. She was going to Europe with her boyfriend. So I decided to call the police for advice. "I think one of my employees has stolen at least $25,000 from our company." I gave them more details and asked what I should do.

"You'll have to lay charges," the officer said. "If you don't, she can leave the country. If you just sue her it'll take too much time. She'll be long gone." A detective and an officer came to the office, and they arrested her and charged her with theft. She wasn't put in jail but was released and ordered not to leave the city. Meanwhile, preparing for the trial, we had all the books audited and were gathering proof.

She chose trial by jury. I sat there in the courtroom and barely recognized the girl who walked in. This girl, who normally dressed rather provocatively, looked like Heidi of the Alps, all fresh-faced and wearing a cute little white dickey. She played it to a T, denying everything, crying "poor me, poor me." It didn't do her any good; they found her guilty. But she only got a year's probation because she was young, it was her first offence (that she'd been charged with), she was from out of town and she had no family (we thought).

Not long after the trial, I got a call — from her dead father! He was in town and had heard his daughter was in some kind of trouble. I said, "But you're supposed to be dead. You and your wife are dead."

"Well," he said, "she does have a lot of stories."

"She certainly does. Just so you know who your daughter is — she's not just a storyteller. She's a thief."

Being on a year's probation didn't stop her from getting a job, which I discovered one day while I was at the Canadian National Exhibition where we had a booth. I was walking around to get the lay of the land, and there, a few booths away from ours, was this girl. I looked at her in disbelief. Not only should she be behind bars, but she's standing there with a big smile on her face, handing out flyers. There was a gentleman standing beside her, so I walked up to him. She saw me, and looked like she was going to faint. "Excuse me," I said. "Do you know who this girl is who's working for you? What did she tell you? That her parents were killed in an accident? Right? Well, I spoke to her father not long ago and he is alive and well. And did she tell you that she was tried in a court of law with theft over $20,000 from my company, found guilty, and is on probation?" I then bid him a good day and walked away.

I never got my money back. What really angered me was after they found her guilty, and I asked about when and how I'd receive the money she stole, the judge said, "We're not a collection agency, Miss Fulcher. You have to sue her civilly to get any money back." There she was, after being found guilty, resuming a normal life with *my* money in her bank account. Who says crime doesn't pay!

This was another instance where our judicial system is just ridiculous. I was so fed up with our government and the process and the rules. Imagine someone saying, "We're not a collection agency." Our company is out over $20,000 and the judge can't even order her to repay the money! I'm now supposed to sue her civilly and go through this whole procedure again? Not likely.

I Am Canadian

The first five years of any business is a struggle, and I think there should be more government support and encouragement of start-ups. I had so many headaches starting my beauty business and the Spa. It was a huge headache when the Human Rights Commission swooped down on my business because one immigrant husband who knew how delicate the human rights issue was at the time decided I should refund his wife's money — and knew the ropes on how to achieve this. That is not how you help small businesses survive. If you watch *Dragons' Den*, you can see that all those new businesses not only need money, they need expert help and support. Some of the ideas for products are amazing. But the sad fact is that many of these entrepreneurs are either going to go to China to manufacture their products, or they'll forget it and the ideas will be picked up by someone in another country. And none of the jobs will go to Canadians. My blood boils when I'm trying to get help with some problem with Bell, Rogers, whoever, and I can't even understand what the person on the phone is saying. Once, they called me three times and left a call-back number and I simply could not understand it. I asked my husband to listen to it and he couldn't understand it either. But if companies are allowed to outsource jobs like that to foreign workers and pay $2 an hour instead of $15 here, of course they're going to take advantage of that. We have to do a lot more to protect our workers because if we don't, in 10 or 20 years from now all the companies will be owned by people in other countries.

I love my country and I'm proud that I'm a Canadian. But I think sometimes we're not helping each other enough, certainly not small businesses. Governments seem to discourage small business by squeezing every last tax penny possible, while big companies send huge amounts of tax-free dollars offshore. Why don't they go after the fat cats!

My father was a good, hard-working man, a labourer, and he would never intentionally offend anyone. But to him, a Chinese person was "Charlie" and an Italian was a "wop." He didn't say it in a derogatory way; he only said it to identify someone. We'd go out to dinner to a Chinese restaurant and my dad would call the waiter Charlie.

Once, when he was in a double room in the hospital with prostate cancer, a Chinese man had the bed next to him. I used to take some cookies or juice from the trolley in the hallways (always asking first, naturally), and this Chinese man complained to his sons. "See Eleanor, she good to her father. She get everything for her dad. You give me nothing, nothing." (I showed his sons where to find the trolley and that it was okay to lift a few things for their dad — just tell the food server.) Anyway, my dad always called his roommate Charlie. "My name is Woo Tong Fu," the man told my dad several times, but my dad just kept calling him Charlie. Oh dear, this double room is never going to work out, I thought. But next thing I knew, Dad and his Chinese roommate got along great. Woo Tong Fu was smart enough to know that my dad didn't have a great capacity with language; Dad was a quiet man, and he never meant to insult. They found a common ground and became buddies — and he grew to accept the name Charlie!

Times have changed and now everything has to be so politically correct, but usually, if you just let people get together and sit down and work it out, it turns out just fine.

Canadians have some of the brightest and best people in every field — but the world doesn't know it and it's up to us to let them know it. For instance, when I was dealing with all the New York and other American agencies, I had to really prove them wrong in their negative attitude toward Canadians. I was constantly promoting our Canadian models because they were right up there with the most beautiful, talented and clever girls in the world. It's up to us to change the attitudes. People think they can take advantage of Canadians; we're not as political and we often won't stand up for ourselves, so they think we're pushovers. The attitude is, Go to Canada and they'll take care of you, you don't even have to work, you'll get all kinds of free stuff, it's easy and cheap in Canada. If someone tries to take advantage of us, we need to stand up and yell, "I'm not going to take this anymore!" We need to raise our collective voices, get feisty, complain. For instance, *The Globe and Mail*, in redesigning their newspaper, decided to drop the daily bridge column, which upset my morning routine. I was really annoyed and phoned them and told them that if they didn't reinstate it, I was cancelling my subscription. Apparently I wasn't the only one to complain, because four days later it was back in the paper. You have to fight for what is right, what you believe in, even if it's for something as small as not allowing someone to cut in front of you in a line. You can do it nicely but firmly. "Excuse me, I was here first. I'm in front of you." But I've seen people let someone push right in front of them and not say anything. You have to stand up for yourself no matter how big or small because it says a lot about you if you don't.

I believe Canadians have to be twice as good as anybody else in order to get noticed on the international scene — and unfortunately, in our own country sometimes. It's not just talent. Look at Justin Bieber, Shania Twain, Paul Anka, Michael Bublé, Celine Dion — Canadians who are huge international stars. You have to be gutsy and you have to believe in yourself. It doesn't matter how many times you have to knock on doors to get attention, you have to be persistent. Learning how to take rejection or deal with failure is important. All the top stars have had some know-it-all agent tell them, "Forget it, it's not your thing, you'll never make it." These huge Canadian/international stars had enough confidence and self-esteem to carry on no matter what obstacles they encountered. I am so proud of each and every one of them — because it's not easy!

CHAPTER 6

SELLING THE BUSINESS

In the 1970s, Eleanor Fulcher was well known as the top Canadian modelling school and agency. The business was so ready to branch out, be franchised, taken across Canada and the U.S., but I never found the right people. Today, with computers, it would have been easier to network, connect with the right people and set up systems, but back then it was just me. I was brainwashed, like all women were, to believe that only men could do certain jobs, like the sales manager I had to let go because a ballgame was more important than his job working with women. I went across Canada once on a lecture series and met so many great, strong women who could have operated a school or agency franchise — and were ready to invest money. They were ready to be entrepreneurs, ready to take risks, get started right away! But I didn't know how to follow through. It would mean I'd have to replace myself — personally train these owners/operators and go to their city and help them start it up, and I was simply not able to be in two places at the same time. I was also trying to raise my family. There's only so much one person can do. I'm sorry I couldn't pursue it then — it was so needed and wanted.

I did try opening a branch in Burlington, which I thought would be a good market because the demographics are spot-on, but it didn't work. Women there were skeptical and I had to spend too much time selling the programs. In Toronto, it pretty much sold itself — once people heard about it and understood what it could do for them, they were ready. I needed someone who lived in Burlington to manage the business, someone who had the patience to build it. It was taking up way too much of my time, so after about three months I gave up on that idea and closed it.

I think women have more realistic expectations in a new business venture. We don't need all the glitz. When men start a business they rent space and immediately have to spend $50,000 on office décor and furniture and so on. Women are content to start with a desk and phone in a basement office. In general, women are more frugal and won't spend a dime until they've earned a dime. Women are more likely to have a support system and ask for help if they need it. Men, on the other hand, think they know the right way — their way — and charge ahead, sometimes blindly. The men I hired? I couldn't tell them anything — they knew everything! I learned the hard way, and it's too bad, because franchising was becoming the big venture — it can be quite profitable. But franchising was very new back then and I didn't have the right connections. My only regret is that I know that there are so many women who would have loved and benefitted from our many programs and especially the Eleanor Fulcher Model of the Year Awards Fashion Show extravaganza.

When the recession hit in 1990 it really affected our business — boom, bang, crash. Ours was the kind of business that flourished when parents and businesspeople had some extra money to enable them to attend our school. When the bottom falls out of the economy, the "extras" or non-essentials are the first to go. That's when the whole thing started to fall apart. I sold our 791 St. Clair Avenue West building to Skills for Change, which was half owned by the government — they're the only ones who had money! Skills for Change was flourishing, and fortunately they were one of the very few businesses at the time looking for more space. You can imagine my surprise when I informed the manager of Skills for Change that I'd be selling the building as soon as possible and she would have a new landlord. She said, "Give me a few hours before listing it, Eleanor." One hour later she called to say they would buy the building immediately. Hallelujah!

I had an incredible archive of 40 years of photos, flyers, booklets and documents in the basement of 791 St. Clair. The library of photos — the ones the media relied on — was incredibly valuable. Priceless really. It was so vast that I hired Katrina, my niece from Switzerland, to help with the task of organizing it — labelling everything, storing it properly. She worked at it for almost a year while living with us. When I sold the building, the new owner let me keep my archive storage space because they didn't need the space immediately. She told me when they needed the space she'd let me know so I could transfer all the files to storage units. Then she went on vacation, and when she came back, all my archives had been thrown out. My life's work — destroyed, tossed in a dumpster, stolen, sold — I'll never know. It devastated me. For the longest time I was depressed, totally crushed, and it still upsets me to think about it. Who did this? I believe it was an employee of Skills for Change. The owner told me he left without notice. Maybe he hated women, especially beautiful women in the modelling field. We'll never know. The police and insurance company tried to track him down to no avail. He just disappeared. At one point they traced him to Vancouver, but once again he disappeared.

We downsized to the 1500 square feet of space I had leased at the Eaton Centre for five years beginning in 1986 when business was flourishing — primarily for our model agency expansion at the time.

Then, on October 31, 1991, I sold Eleanor Fulcher International to Traute Siebert. Traute had been with me for 20 years in different capacities: model, teacher, manager, vice president and friend. We had a two-year agreement. She would pay me so much money if the business was viable — and I would be available to help her at any time. Well, she never once called me for advice. I'd phone her and check on how she was doing, always getting the same answer: "Ev-

Announcing our opening at the Eaton Centre in Toronto, 1986

The sale of Eleanor Fulcher International
to Traute Siebert, 1991

erything's fine." I was delighted. A whole other life was opening up
to me and I was able to relax.

Many years later Traute confessed to me that she cried every night
for two years because of business problems — but she knew she had
to solve them. She felt that if she called me she would lose her confidence to make decisions. She also told me that when she bought the
business her husband said he'd handle the "business end," as she had
no experience. (What did he think she'd been doing for 20 years?)
She told him, "Over my dead body." So she also had something to
prove to her husband. True grit. And it worked! I love that girl.

The night I sold the business, I remember coming home and thinking, Okay, now what? I'd been in the beauty business for 40 years.
I'd been "Eleanor Fulcher" for so long, how could I be anyone else?
When you build a business on your name and suddenly you're no
longer in the industry, you've got to find out who you are other than

Forty years later, in 2000, still going strong!

"the business." But I was ready to do that — excited to do that. I was 56. I had been in the industry since I was 17. It was time.

I certainly didn't think I was "retiring." It was just a new facet of my life, another corner turned. The opportunity to explore other possibilities was to me just incredible. I loved the feeling, and I still do! Instead of "retire," I like the word "rewire." Nothing about the word "retirement" suggests excitement or enthusiasm. It's more like out to pasture, old, "tired." Not me. I like "rewired."

The first day after I sold the business, I flew to Florida to visit my friend Tuula, and by the time I got on the plane, my new life had started. I never again thought, "Who am I now that I'm out of the business?'" I think everyone has to guard against letting their job become their total identity.

Now my life is still so full I don't have time to sneeze. I manage four properties, spend time with my family, visit and keep in touch with extended family and friends, enjoy luncheons, bridge, theatre, my investment club, dinner parties and trips, and stay healthy through good diet, exercise and regular checkups. I keep meticulous records of all my health appointments.

It's so important to take charge of your own health. A few years ago I had what I thought was a bladder infection, which turned out to be far worse — it was cancer. The doctor had missed it, and I probably wouldn't be here today if Bruno hadn't mentioned my problem to a friend, Paul Miller, who happened to be connected to a prominent specialist. One phone call was all it took and it undoubtedly saved my life. They reopened my file and three days later I was on the operating table. When our lives are busy it's tempting to leave things up to the professionals, but we can't do that — we have to be

Bruno and Paul Miller (left), the man who made the phone call that saved my life

Opening doors and making over

:Life is beautiful,
:but it can also be
:a lot of hard work

BY GEORGE GAMESTER
COLUMNIST

So, Eleanor. When did you lose your life?

Seven years ago? Hey, you still look pretty good, considering.

All that work you did, putting together decades of personal and business photographs, videos and writings which you planned to turn into a book.

Yes, your whole life was there in colour-coded boxes. Sitting in an office storeroom. Until . . .

WHOOSH! A clean-up crew mistakenly pitched the whole works into the garbage. Gone forever.

Still makes your blood boil, doesn't it?

But here's the thing, Eleanor. Your story should be told. Because there's so much to it: Beauty. Glamour. Inspiration. Achievement. And fascinating glimpses of Toronto's social history.

So let's do it: The Eleanor Fulcher Story . . .

Where to start? East-end Toronto, of course, where so many intriguing stories begin.

You were poor, weren't you, kiddo? Well, who wasn't? Moving from house-to-house in the gritty Queen-Pape neighbourhood during the Depression, your father earning maybe $5 a day delivering door-to-door for Foster Ice and Fuel.

But you never *felt* poor, did you? Especially at the house on Caroline Ave. where your Norwegian-born grandmother, Tilla Hansen, cooks the Sunday roast and you all gather around the piano for sing-songs after the dishes are done.

Even then, your mom has big ambitions for you. Muriel Fulcher, a three-times-a-week regular at the Joy theatre on Queen St., is such a movie fan she names you after one of her favourite stars, Eleanor Powell.

And since the Hollywood Eleanor is a tap-dance whiz, Mom toddles you off to the Beth Weymes Dance School on Queen St. two years before kindergarten. You might say your working life begins right there.

Work. Very important in the Fulcher family. At Bruce Public School, you're *expected to* be at the top of the class — just as you're expected to turn over a portion of your $3.86 pay from your Saturday job at the Christie-Brown bakery for household expenses.

And when you decide to quit school in Grade 11 at Eastern High School of Commerce for a full time

'I looked around and realized all these clever older ladies, these secretaries, were actually running the office — and earning one-third what their younger, male bosses were getting'
— ELEANOR FULCHER

bright. But university is out of the question. This is 1950, after all, and there are only three traditional career paths for working-class women: Teaching, nursing, secretary.

Soon, you catch on as a clerk at Lever Brothers, $25 a week. Do very well, too. Even then, as a 16-year-old, people begin to notice you. For starters, you're a good-looking girl. You work hard, relate well to people. The older executive secretaries like you, take you under their wings.

Within a year, you're amanuensis to an office hotshot, Bruce Johnson, the guy with the Lipton account. But there's a problem. The boss feels your "look" isn't really suitable for the business world. You resemble a bobby soxer, he says. Perfectly true — since you still wear bobby socks.

So it's off to the Walter Thornton Agency, a sort of modelling school where young women learn how to dress with flair, use makeup properly and deport themselves becomingly. Well! Before long, you're sharing all you've learned with many of your co-workers back at Lever Brothers.

You were happy there. Eleanor. Until the revelation. . . .

"One day, it just hit me. I looked around and realized all these clever older ladies, these secretaries, were actually running the office — and earning one-third what their younger, male bosses were getting.

"I had one of those flashes, you know? I could see the future, and knew if I stayed I'd wind up just like them. I had to get out."

So you quit. Just like that. No safety net. But in your next office job, it's quickly apparent you're smarter than your boss. So you quit again, and wind up — SURPRISE! — at Walter Thornton.

They take to you there. And why not? You're easy on the eyes, have a

words a minute. Before long, the boss signs you to a seven-year, $300-a-month contract as manager of the whole operation. You are 19.

Quite a leap. But only the beginning, really. Though you do well at Thornton, there's a sense of déjà vu — that you'll always be underpaid and under someone's thumb. When your contract ends, you're outta there.

Which is how you wind up on a Bloor St. sidewalk in the spring of 1969, intently scrutinizing passing women. Finally, you see one you want: A dowdy-looking person with bad hair, dull looks and perfect cheekbones.

Her name is Dora, and here's the deal: You offer her a complete makeover, new hairstyle and makeup for no charge. All you want is her permission to show her new look in a before-and-after advertisement.

"Why not?" says Dora — and the Eleanor Fulcher Self-Improvement and Model School is born.

Armed with a $500 loan from a skeptical bank manager, you run photos of Dora's dramatic makeover in a Toronto Star ad, sit back and wait for the phone to ring.

When calls come, you pull an Eddie Murphy routine — answering with a phony voice (the receptionist), then "switching" the call to the proprietor (your real voice) to discuss programs and prices, before consulting your (imaginary) schedule to see if you could fit them in.

Hey, it works. Now all you need is a place to conduct your clinics. And here's where you get another great idea.

The Joseph Bobyk Salon at Bloor and Avenue Rd. is one of the classiest hair-styling establishments in the city. Now you approach Mr. Bobyk with a daring proposal.

nings (when his place is closed) his high-rent location is not earning him a penny. So why not let you use part of the premises after-hours for your beauty school?

In addition to collecting some rent, you suggest he'll also gain customers from the ranks of your clients. To your surprise, Bobyk says yes.

Bingo! You're on your way. And the timing is perfect. For this is the pre-liberation era when women's looks are considered all-important — in school, careers and finding a guy.

Remember? Girdles, waist-cinchers, spike heels, beehive hairdos and hats were *de rigueur*. And to learn all the secrets of feminine success, many women would take classes in makeup artistry, fashion and graceful movement.

And when these women marry and raise families, they will often send their daughters to "finishing schools" such as yours.

Sounds quaint now. But it's a bonanza for you, as your shoestring operation grows through the 1960s and '70s to a multi-faceted business centered in your wholly-owned St. Clair Ave. W. headquarters embracing 55 staff, 2,000 students, and 500 models and actors. Big bucks.

Now, a decade after selling the business, we find our one-time poor girl from Queen-Pape living with her architect husband of 39 years in a

handsome Castle Frank home.

A grandmother now, busy with charity work and socializing with friends dating back to her years of struggle, she still runs across former "Fulcher Girls" wherever she goes.

So tell us, Eleanor: If you were starting out today, would you take the same route?

"Of course not. Today, I'd get a university education, go for one of the professions. It's such a different world now. Women have so much confidence. And so many more doors are open to them." Still, the traditional old doors — hard work, ingenuity, talent — worked pretty well for you.

No, you didn't tap-dance your way to Hollywood to fulfil your mother's dream. But most of your dreams came true.

And any mom can live with that. As 86-year-old Muriel Fulcher might say, when you stop by for one of your mother-daughter visits:

"Ya done good, kid."

DO YOU HAVE A STORY? We're celebrating the extraordinary lives of "ordinary" people. To tell us about an unforgettable person or incident that has touched, changed or enriched your life, call (416) 869-4874 anytime. Or write to me at Gamester's People, George Gamester, Toronto Star, One Yonge St., Toronto, Ont. M5E 1E6. Fax: 869-4322. E-mail: ggamest@thestar.ca

FULCHER PHASES: Eleanor tap-danced from tiny talent shows to glamour days and big biz, touching Toronto lives along the way.

An article in the *Toronto Star* in 2001 by George Gamester, ten years after I sold the business

proactive. Also, it's our natural tendency (though men are worse than women in this respect) to keep our problems to ourselves, but sometimes it's good to talk about them — not only to share resources and support, but also because you never know when a serendipitous comment or meeting can change the course of your life.

If you're a busy person, time fills up. People that are used to being busy will always be busy. I find I almost have to "edit" what I do because I'm interested in everything. I'm tempted to read every book, magazine and newspaper, play every game, go to every play, watch special TV shows. I've learned to be selective. A friend asked me the other day, "Do you like Sudoku?" I said, "I refuse to even try it. I'm afraid of getting hooked because I love games." I only have time in the morning to do the crossword, my bridge column, and read the paper. That's it! If I take on too much I won't have time to do the things that I should be doing.

CHAPTER 7

Some Famous Encounters

Elizabeth Taylor

Elizabeth Taylor was a great beauty and a Hollywood icon, as everyone knows. In the late 1970s, I was privileged to go to her birthday party at the Four Seasons Hotel here in Toronto.

Elizabeth was in Toronto filming a movie called *Between Friends*. They were filming in a big mansion not far from our house, and my friends George Abbott and Larry Wells were involved in the movie. George was responsible for Elizabeth Taylor's makeup. Larry was helping with costume design. When they broke for lunch, George and Larry would come to my house. "Okay," I said to them. "Here's the deal. I give you lunch, you introduce me to Elizabeth Taylor." So when they were throwing a fiftieth birthday party for her at the Four Seasons, they invited me.

It was lovely. The whole room was decorated with streamers, confetti and sequins in mauve and white, her favourite colours.

Elizabeth had a bit of a cold that day so she was holding up a pretty mauve fan against her face so she wouldn't pass along any germs. Only her eyes showed. And what beautiful eyes! They were truly violet — absolutely mesmerizing. She had a beautiful face, but those eyes!

The occasion was also a wrap for the film, so the entire cast and crew were there. Elizabeth could hardly speak from her cold, and when they wheeled out this enormous birthday cake, she could only whisper her gratitude. You could have heard a pin drop in that room. Everyone strained to hear what she was saying before she blew out a couple of candles. Everyone loved her. That's why she was a big star for so long — she was kind and generous and beautiful. The world will never forget her.

Judy Garland

I was on vacation in Manzanillo, Mexico, at the same time as a good friend of mine, Audrey Gostlin, was doing a fashion shoot. Audrey was the editor of the *Star Weekly* fashion section and had flown in with her crew, a top model, hairstylist, makeup artist and photographer and assistant. About eight of us got together for dinner one night, including Audrey's model, hairstylist and makeup artist. We were having a pleasant evening, when someone in our party looked across the room and said, "Hey, Judy Garland is sitting over there!" It turned out the makeup artist and hairstylist at our table knew the guy Judy Garland was with, so we invited them over for a drink. This friend of Judy's started fawning over the model, who was still in full fashion makeup. "Oh, your eyes!" he said. "Darling, they are so beautiful." He went on and on making a big fuss, and it started to annoy me. I mean, he's basically ignoring Judy Garland, just one of the biggest stars in the world.

I suddenly blurted out, "False! Three sets of lashes!" He looked at me a little surprised. Judy got a kick out of this and laughed out loud.

"That reminds me of when I was on a cruise and I decided to wear false eyelashes," Judy said. "I couldn't see what I was doing when I was trying to apply them, so I put my glasses on. I thought I had the lashes on perfectly but when I went to dinner, I discovered they were stuck on my glasses." That broke us all up. She was very funny and could laugh at herself. What you saw was what you got with Judy Garland. What a talent. A true legend.

Speaking of false eyelashes, one night my friend Shirley, who was one of my models, stayed over at my place. I walked into the bathroom and saw a big black thing crawling around in the shower. I thought it was a tarantula, and I screamed! Shirley came running in to see what was the matter. "Oh!" she said. "That's where they went!" The big black thing was her false eyelashes. We both had a great laugh.

Dinner With Shirley Jones and David Cassidy

A good friend of mine, Meryl, was engaged to David Cassidy, the singer and TV star. He and his stepmother, Shirley Jones, were in Toronto taping a Christmas show for CFTO, so Bruno and I invited them out for dinner. We all came back to our house for after-dinner liqueurs.

At this time, our niece Katrina was staying with us for a year. As I mentioned earlier, she'd come from Switzerland to work and to help me organize all our model photo files. Well, I didn't think Katrina would even know who David Cassidy and Shirley Jones were when I told her they were coming to our house later that night. But apparently I was wrong. They were just as popular in Switzerland. "David Cassidy?" she said.

"Yes, he's a singer. He's quite well known."

"*The* David Cassidy? He's coming here?"

So after dinner, we were back at the house having drinks in the living room, when Katrina arrived home. She went right upstairs to her bedroom without even saying hello. I thought, Oh. I guess she decided she didn't want to meet David and Shirley. But half an hour later, she came down, dressed to kill, low-cut blouse, complete fashion makeup, the whole deal. When I saw her I said, "Oh! You're going out! I thought you'd join us for a drink."

"I am joining you for a drink," she said, and without taking her eyes off David, strolled over to him and sat on a little stool beside him. Katrina is a beautiful girl and she has this delightful accent and is using her assets for all their worth, flirting outrageously with my friend's fiancé! David took it in stride; he's used to adulation.

We had such a good time that night. At one point Shirley Jones was trying to remember a tune, and I said, "We have a piano downstairs. Let's go." Her conductor was there with us. We all went downstairs in a party mood and gave the piano a great workout, with everyone performing. What a great evening! When I apologized later for Katrina's flirtatious behaviour, my friend Meryl said, "Don't worry, it happens all the time."

Another time, Meryl took me to see David at the O'Keefe Centre when he starred in *Joseph and the Amazing Technicolor Dreamcoat*. We sat near the front. In the rows ahead of us, there were dozens of groupies. These girls were doing everything but throwing their panties at him! I said, "Meryl, how do you stand it?" She told me she got used to it. But after two or three years, they divorced. I remember thinking, How can a marriage survive, when one partner is on the road most of the time with women falling all over him? So many temptations.

Prince Philip, Duke of Edinburgh

Bruno and I were invited to a gala reception for Prince Philip at the Royal York Hotel. He was doing his walkaround and being introduced to everyone. Bodyguards were everywhere. I was standing with Bruno and one of my models, Lynda Prince, was behind me. Lynda is tall, elegant and gorgeous. Prince Philip approached us and I introduced myself. I gave a quick rundown on my business and pointed out some of our models selling fundraising tickets at the door.

His face lit up. "Oh, really!" We get chatting and he's got his eye on Lynda and says, "Is that one of your models behind you?"

I said, "Oh! Yes, that's Lynda. Lynda, come here. The Duke wants to meet you."

Meanwhile, the Duke's PR coordinator is getting really annoyed because he has to keep things moving with all kinds of other people to meet, and here's the Duke standing talking to us about the modelling business and quite enjoying himself. He indeed has a twinkle in his eyes and is so charming.

His Royal Highness Prince Philip

CHAPTER 8

Fun Times and Pastimes

Oh, To Dance!

I recently read an article called "How the Tango Seduced Me." It was about a woman who'd been shy and reserved all her life and how she is transformed by taking dance lessons and learning how to relax and just "go with it." That's really what we were training our students to do at the school. Having grace and poise is all about relaxing your body and moving naturally. If you do anything often enough, it becomes second nature. And that's what dancing is all about, too.

When I was taking lessons as a young girl, the teacher at Beth Weyms once said, "Now class, look at Eleanor's expression. She's feeling the music." When she said that I understood, because I did feel it. I let the music take over and get into my body and move me. It's not that I was that great a dancer, just that I felt the music, to the point where it was impossible to sit still. I would feel compelled to move. Music can do that and dancing can too, if you let it.

I once dated a dancing instructor and I hated dancing with him because it was so technical and controlled and stiff. He'd be saying, "Stand straight, lean back, put your hand here…" I couldn't stand it. I'm not that kind of dancer. The whole point is to have fun.

I find street dancing fascinating. All these dancers doing rap and hip-hop moves. Wonderful, incredible, creative moves.

To this day I love dancing. I am a total ham on the dance floor. Bruno and I dance well together but he is not what I'd call a good natural dancer. He doesn't let it take over. But he doesn't mind when I break out on the dance floor (within reason!) and enjoy myself. He's sort of like the back-up dancer doing his conservative moves while I'm feeling it.

I had one dance with Andy Body, my choreographer, that was really special. We grew up in the same era and knew all the same moves. One night after a rehearsal for the Model of the Year show, a few of us went to Maxwell's Plum for a drink. Everyone was dancing and Andy said, "C'mon Eleanor, let's have a dance." I'd known Andy for two or three years by that time but we'd never danced together. It was amazing how well we anticipated each other's moves. Everyone cleared the floor and applauded at the end. It was just one of those moments when two dancers fit — and it is truly magical. We have often recalled that moment fondly.

It happened to me again in Mexico. My fiance and I had broken up and I needed to get away for a while, so I took a week off and flew to Acapulco by myself. I met a chap who asked me out to dinner, and we went to a beautiful outdoor restaurant under the stars. The atmosphere was glorious — a perfect evening. Then the orchestra struck up my favourite song, "La Bamba." I don't know if it was the place, the drinks, the mood, the music, the stars, my frame of mind…I don't know what came over me. I could not sit still and got up on the dance floor and started dancing — by myself. And oh, did I dance! Everyone was watching me as the orchestra played on. I was the floorshow. I was so happy. I was totally in the moment and I just let loose; it was the most natural thing in the world. Something in me was released with that dance. I felt free, ready to start a new life. Looking back, I can hardly believe I did that.

Another time I was at the Royal York Hotel in Toronto after judging a beauty contest. There was a photographer there who'd also been one of the judges. His name was Struan Campbell-Smith and he was one of my favourite photographers. Very charming and very European. We were packing up to leave. The orchestra was playing a waltz and he asked me if I'd like to dance. Would I! It was wonderful. He was my kind of partner. We were great together. We covered the floor and danced for two hours. It was another one of those magical times you never forget.

I love to watch my good friends Traute and Cathy dance. They don't think they're very good. But they do their own thing and they're happy, and that's just beautiful. They're letting go and moving whatever wants to move. Cathy does what I call "the move," where she'll throw her leg around a guy's waist and bend back. She first did it when we crashed a staff party on a cruise. I never laughed so hard.

"Nice move," I said to her when she sat down.

"I don't know what came over me," she said. It's so unlike her — she's very conservative normally — but the inspiration was there and she went for it. And why not? Just let go, no matter how you dance or how old you are. Just let it go. Don't be self-conscious and don't take yourself seriously. Get up and move everything that wants to move. Dancing can be so therapeutic. Just do it! Never forget how to have fun and how to laugh. As long as you can dance and laugh, then you're fine.

The Importance of Time Out

I unwind and relax with a favourite movie or song. It can immediately change my mood. Whenever I need comfort – whether I'm stressed, tired or upset about something – I listen to some of my favourite songs, like "Last Date" (Floyd Cramer), "Lady in Red" (Chris deBurgh), "Try" (Blue Rodeo), just about anything by Frank Sinatra, "I Will Always Love You" (Whitney Houston), "I Will Survive" (Gloria Gaynor), and so many others. Or I might watch a favourite movie. I love *Forrest Gump*, *Erin Brockovich*, *Good Will Hunting*, *Illegally Blonde*...just good stories. No violence, no car crashes. It's interesting what makes you connect to a certain song or movie. It's something deep inside you and if you look closely, it can tell you something about yourself. It's worth it to think about how you connect to certain things, and more importantly, write down your favourites.

Speaking about being connected, I think people would be far better off if they *dis*connected from all these devices – iPads, iPods, computers, iPhones, Blackberries and so on. You see people in restaurants or waiting rooms and they can't go two minutes without texting or checking their email or talking. The line between "work" and "leisure" has been blurred in the past few years. Now, people can be reached at all hours of the day and night, wherever they are, even on what's supposed to be a vacation. There's no escape! Everyone needs some down time. When I was running my business and the children were young, I had long, busy days, and I would be exhausted when I got home. I'd walk in the door and the kids would be all over me, demanding my attention, wanting to play, show me something, do things with me. I sometimes found it overwhelming and it was because I hadn't had time to switch from being a businesswoman to being Mommy. I told my doctor this and he said,

"This is what you must do. The children have to understand that when you come in the door, first of all you need ten quiet minutes to sit down with a glass of red wine, and they are not to disturb you during that time." And it worked!

Being Silly

I love to get silly, especially with my girlfriends. I was reminiscing the other day about Heather Jenkinson and I going to a laundromat in Bobcaygeon with a thermos of Black Russians (our favourite cocktail) and getting completely pickled while we waited for the laundry to dry. I remember trying to fold all these bedsheets and finally just throwing them up in the air and jumping under them. We thought it was hilarious and we laughed and laughed.

Going to Pot

Cathy Richardson and I have been friends since our teens. One year we were in North Palm Beach, Florida, with another friend. We all went walking on the beach every morning, and this particular morning we saw a great big bundle wrapped in garbage bags. Cathy said, "You don't think this could be what they were talking about on the news this morning? The police said the boat was near here."

I said, "What do you mean? What boat?"

"The police stopped a boat because they thought there was marijuana onboard." What they used to do, apparently, was when they saw the police or coast guard approach, they would just dump their cargo overboard. This cargo was pot.

In those days we knew very little about marijuana. We were young and naïve. My other friend, who I'll just call L for this story, had a sarong around her bathing suit. "Let me borrow your sarong," I said.

She took it off and gave it to me, and I poked a hole in the bundle and pulled out a big handful of this weed-like substance, and wrapped it in L's sarong.

A guy was jogging along the beach, muscles galore, and I said to him, "Excuse me. Do you think you could help us drag this bundle up to our car, because we think that it might be something important. We're going to phone the police and see if this is what they've been looking for." So for some reason, he didn't question that. He just hauled it up on his shoulder, carried it up to the car and put it in the trunk.

Then we phoned the police. I told them we found this bale on the beach and it might be what they're looking for. The police arrived shortly, and we showed them this great big bale in the trunk of the car. They said, "What's this hole here?"

I lied. "I don't know. That was there."

They said, "Thank you very much for calling." They put it in the police cruiser and drove away. Later on the plane home, I was telling this story to a fellow passenger and he said, "Are you crazy? You called the police? That much pot would be worth about $250,000 on the street." Right — we're really going to hit the streets and sell pot!

We'd never even seen pot before, so we didn't know what to do with it. It looks like weeds. We thought what we'd do is dry it out first. So we put it in the microwave, and that didn't work too well, so then we put it in the oven. Then the whole place smelled of the stuff. Well, that's not too good. We had some of it on the windowsill, trying to get the sun to dry it. I said, "We'll put it in the Cuisinart when it's dry. We have to get it powdered."

I said I'd go to the store and get some cigarette papers, because I know I've seen them do this, where they roll it into these cigarette papers. Trying to act casual, I went to the store and bought milk and bread and butter and all this stuff, and by the way, cigarette papers.

It was dried out by this time, so we put the pot in the Cuisinart to grind it up so we could roll it. L is having nothing to do with any of this, but Cathy and I were totally committed. This is fascinating. We're really into it. We've heard so much about it and we're going to try this for once in our lives.

We were having no luck trying to get the pot rolled up in the cigarette paper. All of a sudden, L walked in the kitchen, looked at us and said, "I can't stand this any longer!" She took a paper and some pot and went, zip zip zip. "There!" Rolled it up like a real pro.

We looked at her in utter astonishment. "Where did you learn to do that?"

"I have friends who smoke pot. No big deal." Then she handed it to us and left. Cathy and I were excited by this time: we're finally going to try this.

Everyone smoked cigarettes in those days, the late '50s. But Cathy wasn't even a social smoker. We lit this thing, and I took a drag and handed it to Cathy. We passed it back and forth, standing in the kitchen in our bathrobes, no makeup, and rollers in our hair. What a vision. When it was finished, Cathy said, "I don't feel any different. Do you?"

I said, "No, I don't either. I don't feel anything."

Now, as I mentioned, Cathy is quite conservative, very proper. She was always concerned about her neckline being too low and showing too much cleavage, so she would sew a piece of lace onto a V-shaped top. As I mentioned, she was Miss Toronto in 1954 and was a finalist in 1955 in the Miss Universe pageant. She's a real stunner!

Anyway, Cathy went to her room. I went to my room. We were getting ready to go out to dinner. About ten minutes later she came into my room, and she's stark naked! She stood at the doorway, put her hand on her hip, and said, "I still don't feel any different. Do you feel any different?"

I just looked at her incredulously. Proper Cathy! "Oooh, no, I don't feel any different, either." She'd totally lost all her inhibitions but didn't realize it.

So we went to dinner. Now, Cathy is a delicate eater. She nibbles. We ordered steak, the two of us. This is just an observation of how pot affects people in different ways. I have a fairly good appetite, but as I was about to cut the steak, I suddenly couldn't stand the thought of eating anything. My appetite and sense of taste was totally gone. Never had that experience before or since in my life. Couldn't even bring it up to my mouth. Now, Cathy, on the other hand, was eating like there's no tomorrow. She devoured her steak in record time and looked at my plate and said, "Aren't you going to eat your steak?"

I said, "I can't. I have no appetite at all."

"Well, in that case…." This steak was at least 8 oz. She reached across and stuck her fork in my steak and plunked it on her plate, and proceeded to eat my whole steak too.

We did a lot of funny things with that little bit of pot. Later that evening we took a little of it to some other friends who were celebrating their anniversary. I saw this friend recently and asked, "C, do you remember the day that we brought you some pot?"

She said, "Oh, do I remember it, Eleanor! My God, we smoked the two cigarettes you gave us and we had the best sex we've ever had! It went on and on and on. That was the best anniversary present you could have ever given us!" All these years later we're talking about this! But that was then and this is now.

The Ouija Board

At Johnny Franciotti's farm in Bobcaygeon, where Bruno and I would visit on many weekends, we girls would get into the Ouija board. It was all the rage at the time — ghosts and the spirit world.

Johnny Franciotti and Heather Jenkinson.
Johnny owned Maxwell's Plum, a nightclub
in Toronto and the scene of many fun times,
including my 40th birthday party.

It was supposed to read your mind and spell out messages from "the other side." One night Johnny and Bruno snuck up onto the roof while we girls were playing with the Ouija board. Suddenly we heard a tapping noise on the roof. We thought it must be the spirit world trying to contact us. "Did you hear that?" Tap, tap. We were mesmerized. Then all of a sudden we hear this loud crash, which turned out to be Bruno falling off the roof. So much for ghosts and spirits!

Bridge

Everyone needs a hobby. I never had time for hobbies before I sold the business, but now I do, and I am hooked on bridge. Four of us meet Mondays for lunch and bridge and it's wonderful. Total escapism.

I think in some ways bridge is a lot like life. When you're learning bridge, one of the fundamentals they teach you is to know when to pass. Sometimes you just have to get out of a mess and cut your losses — just as in life.

Bridge is also like business. If you get something worthwhile, you can bid it. Outbid everyone else. You know it's yours. And it's much like that in business. If you've got something going, don't let anyone put you down. Some people will try to bluff and intimidate you, like Gary Carter tried to do to me. Bridge teaches you to believe in what you hold in your hands, and run with it.

I enjoy bridge and I like the challenge but I am not addicted — but many are. If any one of my partners ever started seriously criticizing

My dear friend, former model/employee and bridge partner Barb Bell

how I was playing, I'd just stop. It's a game. Yes, we often analyze the play but never place blame. It's meant to be fun and relaxing.

Often on Thursday nights my friend Barb Bell and I play duplicate bridge at the Toronto Bridge Club. Afterwards the results are posted so everyone knows who came first, second and third, as everyone plays the same boards. Barb and I always leave before the results are announced because we're playing with top players. She'll say, "Eleanor, I think we did really well," and I'll say, "You think?"

She'll say, "We're fourth from the bottom," and I say, "Well, that's an improvement." We have actually on rare occasion come second or third — what a high!

By the way, Barb was one of my former models and my bookkeeper for many years. She still looks sensational 50 years later. (She's 70 and looks 40.) She volunteers in an annual fashion show and luncheon at the Thornhill Country Club. I make sure I take lots of pictures of her just to keep her husband, Carson, on his toes!

The women in my Monday bridge group take turns hosting, so

My Monday bridge group. *Left to right*: Audrey Bynoe, Cathy Richardson, Bev Valentine and me

My housekeeper of 20 years, Lilia, prepares a great spread for our bridge group

once a month we meet at my house. All are great cooks except me. I am not passionate about cooking. Early on it got to be a job trying to keep up with my friends in the kitchen. So after a few months, I advised my friends that what they were eating that day at my house is what they'd be served every time we met at my house: a great cold buffet, which my housekeeper of 20 years, Lilia, loves preparing. She fixes about ten varieties of appetizers, tea sandwiches and sweets. So now I don't worry when my friends serve wonderful, tasty lunches. When they come to my house, they are more than happy with Lilia's spread. Problem solved.

The Spinach Soufflé That Wasn't

Speaking of food — I love to entertain, but as I mentioned, I am not a great cook. My son, Marcus, is a fabulous cook. Marcus always says, "Mom, you don't have any passion for cooking, no love." I answer him, "You never starved growing up, did you?" I admire his passion for cooking but I don't share it. I am not going to traipse around to three different butchers in search of the perfect veal cutlet. But it is an art and I so appreciate the time and effort that goes into it.

Before we adopted our children, Bruno and I lived in a lovely one-bedroom apartment at Bathurst and Eglinton. One night I had a dinner party that I'll never forget. Bruno's dinner-party philosophy is to kick things off with a good stiff first drink, which he certainly did on this occasion. Everyone was in the living room having a good time while I was in the kitchen preparing dinner! I had planned the menu to include, among other dishes, a spinach soufflé. I'd never actually made a soufflé before but I had the recipe, the picture and the ingredients. If you can read you can cook, right? I had my soufflé recipe on the kitchen table when my old, dear friend Gordon (Cathy Richardson's husband) came in, having had a couple of Bruno's drinks, and proceeded to park himself right on top of my soufflé recipe. He started telling me what a wonderful friend I was. He was feeling philosophical and nostalgic. I didn't want to be rude and tell him to get off my recipe and leave me alone to get dinner ready, so I thought, Who needs a soufflé anyway — I'll just serve the spinach, nice and simple, and just chatted with Gordon for a while.

Now, I had never cooked spinach before either. I don't even like spinach. But the soufflé sounded good — I'd even bought a special serving soufflé dish. Having abandoned the soufflé idea, I put the spinach in a pot, added water, put it on the stove, and got the rest of the dinner ready. When I next checked the spinach, all I saw was just a tiny little blob of green! The spinach had shrunk down to next to nothing. What had happened to that beautiful picture in the cookbook? Anyway, it was too late to do anything but serve it, but instead of putting it in a little side dish I put it in the new soufflé dish. (By this time all logic is gone at this dinner party.) I passed it around the table after serving the other items. Everyone peered down at this pathetic little hunk of green and murmured something like, "Oh, I couldn't, thanks. I'm not that hungry." If they'd taken even a teaspoon there'd have been nothing left for anyone else, it was that minuscule an amount — barely enough for one person, let alone six. The dish went all around the table, untouched, and arrived back in front of me.

In later years, I always made sure I had a helper at dinner parties so I could be with my guests and not be stuck in the kitchen. I used to hear everyone laughing and talking in the living room and really felt left out. If you invite people to your house, the most important thing is not the food; it's people. Some people get so caught up with the cooking thing that they miss the whole point of getting together.

I do Thanksgiving ham and Christmas turkey with the whole Arnold clan. Everyone likes some traditions and they all look forward to these special occasions at Papa and Nana's (yes, that's Bruno and me!). Tradition is important. Families need these times together. Life is so fast paced, everyone going in different directions. So these special occasions are important, and always remembered with great fondness by everyone.

The Bridal Shower — and Murphy's Law

Around 1970 my PR assistant, E, was getting married, and I wanted to throw her a shower. I really don't care for standard showers and I wanted to make this one really special. Because I also hated surprise parties (remembering my thirteenth!), I asked E outright what would make it special for her. "I want to give you a shower. What would you like? Anything — you name it."

"Well…I want to have Clint Eastwood do a striptease." We laughed, but in the back of my mind I thought Okay, I'm going to ask my friend, Al Dubin, who did PR for Warner Brothers and knew all these stars, if he could get Clint Eastwood to show up! Nothing ventured, nothing gained. Doing a striptease was probably not going to happen, but maybe he'd pop in if he was in town.

"Right," I said to E. "What's your second choice?"

"Okay. Before I get married I want to see a blue movie."

A blue movie was very risqué back then, something you heard about but which was certainly not readily available. How would I get my hands on a blue movie? Clint Eastwood doing a striptease almost seemed like the easier bet!

I phoned Al and asked if he could get Clint Eastwood for us. Al said he would probably do it for kicks, but Clint wasn't going to be in town when I was holding the shower. (I missed him by one week!) Oh well — at least I tried. But now I had to get my hands on a blue movie. I thought of a couple I knew. They were the "go-to" people if you ever needed something "in" or a little offbeat, so I went to my friend B and asked, "Where would I get a blue movie? Is it possible to rent them?"

"Oh no, Eleanor, you can't rent these things."

Oh. Looked like we were going to have a boring old standard shower after all.

"But," he continued, "I have one you can borrow." I think the title was The Green Door or something.

"Great!" I said, "E will be thrilled."

My friend even offered to hook up his VCR to my TV in our upstairs den, so we'd be all set.

I invited all my staff to the shower and ordered in lots of food and refreshments. My housekeeper would take care of serving the food and cleaning up, and I had champagne cooling in the fridge. By the morning of the shower I had everything organized.

But within a few minutes everything went off the rails!

It started with my not being able to find the housekeeper — my live-in housekeeper. I thought she must have forgotten something and gone out to the store, but as the morning wore on, I realized she had just disappeared. I was frantic — I had all these people coming and so much to do to get ready. My mom and dad were going to babysit Angela and Marcus, who were very young, so I drove them up to my parents' home and rushed back to the house to focus on the shower.

My friend B arrived with the blue movie and the VCR and I took him up to the den so he could get it set up. He told me it would take a few minutes and to leave him there to figure it out. So I went back downstairs. The doorbell rang. It was the lady from the Catholic Children's Aid Adoption Services. A day early!

The Children's Aid visited us once in a while to see how Angela and Marcus were doing — in reality, they were checking up on their home life and making sure everything was okay. I had booked our appointment with this lady for the day after the shower, and here she was at my door. "Oh!" I said, "I wasn't expecting you until tomorrow." She checked her book and said, "Oh sorry. I looked at the wrong day. Well, I'm here now. It won't take long." I had no choice but to invite her in.

It might have worked out okay — we could have had a short meeting and she'd be gone, except my friend started yelling at me from upstairs, "Eleanor! Come up here quick — I need you!" I excused myself and went up and here he was, a very successful businessman in a suit fiddling around with the TV and VCR, behind the TV with all the wires going here and there, trying to fix what he had thought would take no time at all. "Just tell me when it's a clear picture." I can't believe what I'm seeing — even though it was crooked and sideways and fuzzy. Good grief! Meanwhile, I've got the Children's Aid lady sitting downstairs. The whole situation was unbelievable. I thought, She's going to take my kids away from me if she discovers this!

Off I go downstairs and make the lady comfortable and offer her a cup of tea. I'm a wreck! With the tea made, I start to walk to the living room tray in hand, and I trip, and the teapot, cups, cookies — everything — goes flying. Tea spills everywhere, cookies are all over the place, and I'm down on the floor mopping up this mess while the lady's standing over me saying, "Who keeps yelling at you from upstairs?" I try to explain that a friend of mine is trying to set up some home movies as I'm having a bridal shower later.

Finally — finally — she leaves, my friend B gets the blue movie set up, the caterer drops off the food and the girls start arriving, looking drop-dead gorgeous in beautiful evening wear — about 20 of them. I advised them that I had no housekeeper so they'd have to help themselves. I put out boxes of food and got the champagne going. By this time, I needed a drink!

I got the movie going upstairs in the den and everyone was having a good time. I never did see the movie — once in a while I'd peek in on them all laughing and giggling.

Then there was a knock at the door. It's the police. Oh my God, I thought, they've found out about the blue movie. We're all going to be arrested. It was illegal to have these movies in those days. I could just imagine the photo in the newspapers the next day: Eleanor Fulcher and models, handcuffed and behind bars. "Ma'am, I'm sorry to disturb you," the policeman said politely, meanwhile checking out all these beautiful women strolling by the door, "but there's a car blocking your neighbour's driveway and I need you to move it."

"Oh, no problem officer," I said, relieved, and then feeling like some explanation was needed for all the dressed-up women and the laughter coming from upstairs, I added, "I'm having a bridal shower. And we're watching family movies. Very funny movies." Right!

The car was moved, but then one of the girls got sick. She wasn't used to drinking champagne. I told her if she was going to be sick to please not be sick in the house; to go outside. Next thing I know there's another knock at the door and it's three cops. Obviously the first one informed the others, "Guys you won't believe this place. Come and check out all these beautiful women." I thought, If they ask to come inside, that's it. We'll all get arrested. But all they wanted was to tell me that there was a girl outside who was very sick. I looked out and saw these officers huddled around her. "Yes, thank you officers. I'm afraid she's eaten something that didn't agree with her." Right.

The police finally left and I at last sat down and started to relax. I thought, Yes, it's the worst day of my life but now it's over. Nothing else could happen. I got past the disappearing housekeeper, the Children's Aid lady showing up, the blue movie fiasco, the tea disaster and the police showing up. The girls were enjoying the blue movie, laughing, enjoying the food out of the boxes, everything's good...

Except I was wrong. The worst day of my life was far from over. The phone rang. It was my dad, from the hospital. Angela had broken her arm. "She was playing on a swing and fell off."

"Do what you have to do, Dad," I said. "I've got this shower going on and you're right there at the hospital, so tell them to go ahead and put the cast on and I'll be there as soon as possible."

He phoned back a few minutes later and said, "They won't do anything until you sign the release form as the mother, and they want you here right away."

"You're the grandparent! They won't let you do it?"

"Nope. Until you as the mother sign the form, they won't set her arm."

I couldn't believe it. I told the girls, "Just carry on without me. I have to go to the hospital." I called a cab and went down to the hospital, still in my hostess gown, which immediately made me the enemy among the nurses. I sensed the "Well, it's about time you showed up" kind of attitude. I signed the form and said to my dad, "Dad, I really have to get back to the shower. My housekeeper didn't show up and I'm needed. I'll go home, say goodnight to the girls, lock up and be right back."

I got a cab back to the house, said goodbye to the girls, locked the house, and cabbed it back to the hospital. It's now about one in the morning. My parents left and I stayed in Angela's room the whole night. Angela was fine and had her arm in a cast and a sling, but a little girl in the next bed was lying down and hadn't eaten her dinner. So I buzzed a nurse and asked why, and was told that they were too busy to feed her as she wasn't hungry when they had tried. So I ended up feeding this child, helping her to sit up long enough to take some food — she couldn't even sit up on her own. We desperately need hospital volunteers who could do this simple chore. If only I had the time!

Angela and I went home about 8 a.m., and after putting her to bed, I started tidying up the mess from the shower. About 9 a.m., my housekeeper arrived at the door. "Where have you been?!" I shouted.

"Oh, my boyfriend and I decided that we wanted to get married, so we did!"

"You decided to get married yesterday. You knew I was throwing a shower yesterday but you picked that day to get married." I was livid. I said, "You've got five minutes to get your stuff together and leave before I lose it!" What was she expecting? Congratulations?

And by the way, I never did see the blue movie!

CHAPTER 9

GIVING BACK

There are so many needy causes that it is important that those of us who enjoy a good life should give something back to society. I helped out where I could.

Swiss Canadian Chamber of Commerce

My husband is Swiss and belongs to the Swiss Canadian Chamber of Commerce (SCCC). They wanted to raise scholarship funds, so *he* volunteered *me* to help with fundraising. He said I'd be great for the job — God bless him! They needed approximately $200,000. At that point I didn't know anything about fundraising, but I ended up as the chair, with a committee of eight. We'd meet at my house every week. You quickly find out who the workers are. They're the ones on the phone getting things done, getting commitments. Others are just putting in time.

The SCCC held an annual ball. As part of our fundraising efforts, we organized a silent and live auction to be held in conjunction with this event. Everyone loved it. We asked one of our committee members, Bill Mawhinney, who was the PR guy at Swiss Air for years, if he could persuade Swiss Air to donate a trip to Switzerland for the live auction. They did. Bill actually took an auctioneering course so he could promote this prize. "Do I hear $10,000, $10,000, $10,000 going once...*Sold!!*" He was amazing. We also got lots of donations for the silent auction — clothes, furs, you name it. Someone bid about $20,000 for the trip to Switzerland — much more than it was actually worth. But that's how auctions go sometimes. Everyone knows it's for a good cause and they're in the right spirit. (A couple of drinks helps too!)

It was a great experience and a huge success. I got to know our committee very well. In fact, one of the committee members, Cecile, ended up working for Bruno. He was looking for a Girl Friday part time, and I mentioned that Cecile would be great. She had earned my respect in spades. Not only had she impressed me with her attention to detail, she had stood up for herself when another committee member questioned something she had submitted in a financial report and kind of dismissed it in front of everyone. The next week, Cecile retaliated and made sure everyone knew she was right, with all the documents to back her up, and she did it in such a classy manner that I thought, Good for you! She wasn't looking for a job at that time but I thought she might like something part time so I suggested she see Bruno. Within a month she was working for my husband full time. She loved it and several years later is still his full-time assistant, taking care of important details so Bruno is free to handle his end of the business without worry. She's a gem. What a great fit Cecile turned out to be.

Volunteer for something. You never know!

999 Queen Street West

999 Queen Street West was a famous address in Toronto. It was known as 999, an institution for the insane or mentally retarded. I decided that, busy or not, I should do some volunteer work, and thought about where I could be most helpful. Good mental health is such an important issue and was in the papers a lot and still is. So I set up a meeting with the board of directors at 999 and proposed a program that I thought might be helpful to their patients. Mental health has a lot to do with self-image, self-esteem and self-confidence, and I thought many of the patients would benefit from some of our training. The board said, "Great idea. Let's give it a try." I designed a five-week program, once a week for two hours.

My first day, the administrators assigned me 25 doubting patients and set me up in their gym. The lady in charge said, "Have fun," and left. There I was alone with 25 "inmates" in this big gymnasium. I had a moment of uneasiness and then just plunged in.

I had a fitness routine that I followed when I led my classes, so I automatically started to demonstrate all the exercises. We did some exercises for the arms and the legs, and then we came to the neck muscles. This exercise featured blowing an imaginary feather around a room. With chin up, you pursed your lips and walked around the room, following your imaginary feather, keeping it up in the air. It was a good stretch for the neck and very good for posture but it looked pretty strange when you were doing it.

"All right, ladies," I said, "this is for the neck muscles. You blow an imaginary feather around like this...." And I demonstrated. "Now, don't let anyone see you doing this, or they're going to think you're cra—" I stopped myself in the nick of time.

But not quite. One of the patients yelled, "Or we'll be in here another ten years!"

Then everyone started to laugh. I cracked up. They knew very well what I was about to say. Everyone was laughing, and it was wonderful. It was the best thing that could have happened because it broke the ice. From that point on, I had them. They were comfortable with me. When you can laugh together, you can work together.

After that, they all showed up enthusiastically for every class. Everyone in the institution wanted to join because they could hear us having a good time. One day we were doing nails when a gay patient came in and said, "Miss Fulcher, I don't know why they won't let me join your class."

I said, "Oh, come on in. It's okay. We're doing nails." I set him up with everything and he was in seventh heaven. He'd come up to me wiggling his newly painted fingernails. "Look, Miss Fulcher. What do you think of this colour?" The others were very comfortable with him, so he joined our group.

Another time we were having a makeup class. I was working with a girl who was extremely religious and was very reticent about getting made up. I said, "C'mon, Susan, let's just try a few things. A little bit of blush here would be nice, and just a touch of eyebrow pencil... Let's try this lipstick..." I was hoping to get her out of herself because she was very withdrawn. Well, she did start to relax and enjoy herself and I was so pleased that we seemed to be making progress, when a staff member appeared at the door and motioned to me. "Susan has a visitor," she said. "Her priest." Oh oh. Susan screamed and jumped under the table — and wouldn't come out.

I got down on my hands and knees and talked to her under the table. "What's wrong?"

"I can't let him see me like this! What will he think? What's he going to say!" She was truly panicky.

I grabbed a jar of cold cream and ducked back down under the table to talk to her. "You look fine. Don't worry. But here's some cream if you want to remove a little of that blush." I went out to see the priest in the hall and said, "Susan is a little busy at the moment, but if you'll just wait in the lounge…" Then I went back under the table and got this girl cleaned up for her meeting with the priest. What timing!

During another session, I was teaching them fashion. Here are these patients wearing a uniform — some sort of smock — and I'm talking about fashion! But they'd be getting out of there one day, I assumed, and would need to know the basics. I was in the middle of teaching, and suddenly one of the patients said, "Well, my boyfriend likes me to wear pink."

Then another girl from the other side of the room responded, "You don't have a boyfriend."

"I do so have a boyfriend."

"Do not."

"Do so. We had sex every day when I was out."

Oh dear, I thought. I think I'm losing this class.

"You haven't even had sex. You don't even know what sex is!"

"Girls, girls. Now look, let's get back — " I may as well not have been there. They were not listening to me. They went from fashion and clothing to boyfriends and sex.

Somehow I got through that class, but I thought for future programs it might be best to eliminate the fashion segment.

The program was a huge success. The ladies loved it and I believe it really helped them gain self-confidence and feel better about themselves.

I learned much more from the girls at 999 Queen Street than they learned from me. It made me aware of the importance of never prejudging anyone. I went in thinking I'd be working with people with their heads hung low, behaving erratically, and most likely mentally retarded. I was so wrong. Some of them were so smart they would amaze me. They just had some problems and their brains weren't working the way we thought they should. 999 was where the system put people that didn't fit the norms of society. It's closed now, thank goodness. Today people with mental illness can be treated with medication and other forms of therapy. Some, unfortunately, are imprisoned — certainly not the answer. There has to be a middle ground somewhere. I recently attended a fundraising dinner for Healthy Minds Canada. Apparently one in five Canadians will experience a mental illness in their lifetimes. Help is available.

Variety Village

In 1994 I got involved with Variety Club, the fundraising arm of Variety Village in Toronto. At the time, Variety Club was run mostly by men, and they thought it was time to bring some women into the picture. My friend Al Dubin was very involved with Variety and said one day, "Eleanor, we really need women to have a higher profile in this organization. Do you think you could come up with something?" I suggested I could organize a luncheon honouring outstanding women and Al agreed, but he added, "You don't have to make money. We just need to have a luncheon for the ladies — high profile, good publicity, maybe break even."

I said, "Al, you're talking to the wrong lady. If I'm not going to raise money, I'm not going to do the luncheon. You need money for Variety and we're going to raise it." I managed to persuade four friends who were highly successful businesswomen to join the committee. What a team we were. I loved working on it; it was such fun. We told all our friends and associates to invite their friends, and soon it became a very popular semi-annual event and grew bigger every year; we had a following of about 500 women. We had a head table

With Bluma Appel, left, and Fiona Reid at a Variety Club Diamond
Luncheon

The Diamond Awards Luncheon brochure, 2002

and a guest speaker — always a high-profile woman of course. Each
speaker was presented with a very special diamond award pin —
which my diamond expert friend, Cathy Richardson, had designed
by her favourite jeweller — a heart with a diamond in it. Perfect.

The Diamond Award Luncheon honoured women who had made

A photo in the Toronto Sun, August 18, 2002. Me and Variety Club supporter Louis Jannetta.

a significant contribution to society and in particular to worthy charities and causes. Some of the honorees included Maureen Forrester; broadcast journalist Valerie Pringle; Sharon Hampson of Sharon, Lois and Bram; Diane Dupuis, the director of Famous People Players; Global TV's Susan Hay; Ann Mirvish; the Honourable Lieutenant Governor Hilary Weston; Shirley Douglas; Marilyn Lastman; Jeanne Beker, and many more. For years it was held at the Royal York Hotel's Imperial Room. The tickets were about $75 and if a company wanted to be a sponsor and have their logo on the program etc., the cost was $3500. It was always a sell-out.

I was very happy to have had so much to do with Variety, because I needed to give back to the community. I'd been so busy running my business and raising a family that I had no time for charity work. Most of the women of my generation had married young and were involved with charities, not business. I'd always thought, One day my time will come, and sure enough it did — when I sold the business and had some breathing space. I still had tons of energy, too, and welcomed an outlet for it. I simply redirected my energy. I used my organizational skills and contacts and tried my best to get the job done well. It felt great to be part of it. I chaired the Variety Club Diamond Award Luncheon for ten years.

Chester Village

After I sold the business in 1990 I got involved with Chester Village, a non-profit long-term care facility. It was a logical choice, because my mother was a resident there. She had not recovered from my dad's death and her health started to decline, and at one point she was in the hospital. Her doctor recommended she go directly to Chester Village from the hospital instead of coming to my home, as she required 24-hour care, and she was ultimately happy with the arrangement. (In those days whatever the doctor said, you did it.) The building was at Broadview Avenue and Danforth Avenue, five minutes away from my house, which was a great comfort to her. I was there every other day. Soon they asked me if I'd be on one of their committees, and that's how it usually starts — you volunteer for

Forbes West and I worked on the Chester Village fundraising committee.

one committee and they find out you're pretty good and you know what you're doing. Having run my own business for 30 years I was used to taking charge and making things happen. Even though it was volunteer work I put my whole heart into it. Otherwise there's no point.

Being a businesswoman I quickly picked up on how ineffective the management was at Chester Village. I believed the person in charge was not at all qualified other than being able to deal with the unions. He didn't know any of the residents' names and seemed totally indifferent. He'd go into his office and keep the door shut most of the time. I was annoyed. My idea of a good manager for a nursing home is someone who cares about people. "Hi Tom, how are you today? What are you up to?" That kind of person.

I visited for many years attending to my mother and helping with fundraising. Then, when I was nominated to the board of directors, I felt the least I could do was try to make some of the top people accountable. One man in charge of the board meeting agenda actually said we couldn't deal with something I wanted to discuss because it hadn't been put on the agenda! Whose agenda?

Some of the residents would come to me for help, because they'd see me coming and going all the time. Once, a woman told me that she'd bought her mother three new towels, which her mother loved, and just a week later, they'd gone missing. She said she had gone to the management about it and was told they didn't have time to deal with three towels. In actual fact, it was easy to deal with three missing towels because there were only two people in housekeeping looking after the laundry, so that would be a good place to start.

Now, three towels may not be a big deal to the management, but it was indicative of something a lot more serious — the fact that if they weren't willing to investigate the little things, they also weren't willing (or able) to deal with the big issues. I got the same reaction when I enquired about the towels. "Really, Eleanor, I don't have time to be worrying about this."

At the next board meeting, I knew one of the senior staff members was going to be asking for $40,000 in backup supplies for the millenium. This was 1999 and everyone was worried about computers crashing — Y2K — when the date turned to 2000. So I stood up at this meeting and said, "You can't find three towels — and you want us to give you $40,000?" His face went red. I told the rest of the people in the meeting the story about the towels and ended with, "So do you think the staff doesn't know that management doesn't care about supplies? They're just going to go in and take whatever they want — no one cares about missing anything." It certainly shook things up. The next meeting, he had a key around his neck — the only key to the storage room where all the supplies were to be kept.

He was not a bad person. In fact, at the annual Christmas party we'd have a rare old time with him playing the piano and me singing. One Christmas party was especially memorable.

One year, a true legend was temporarily living at Chester Village — the internationally adored contralto, Maureen Forrester. I knew that from time to time she'd had bouts of dementia and she was waiting for some renovations at another facility, but she was at Chester Village over Christmas when we were having our annual party. As the party was getting underway, I noticed she wasn't downstairs with the rest of the staff and residents, so I suggested to the manager that we invite her down to the singalong.

"Oh no," he said, "I promised the family I wouldn't put her through that."

Put her through that? Singing was her life, her love! It wasn't right. This was Christmas and she's living here. So — do I listen to anyone when they're talking nonsense? No. So I went up to her room.

"We're having our Christmas party, Maureen. How would you like to come down and have a singalong with us? Maybe you'd even like to sing."

"Oh, I'd love to!" she said excitedly. "Wait till I get dressed."

When she came down, the manager grabbed me by the arm quite forcefully and said, "She cannot sing."

I said, "Sue me," and I walked past him with Maureen, went up to the microphone, introduced her, and everyone in the place went nuts. I said, "What would you like to sing, Maureen? You name it."

She started to sing "Silent Night" in her lovely voice, and it was beautiful. Everyone in the room was spellbound. But halfway though, she stumbled on the lyrics. I was right beside her and when I could see that she was having problems — she just stopped for a second and couldn't quite remember the lyrics — I jumped right in. I started to sing with her and gestured for everyone to join in, and we all sang with her. Everyone loved her; they were standing and applauding and cheering. Maureen was so happy. There was hardly a dry eye in the room.

That moment when we all sang with Maureen Forrester — these are the moments that life is made of, and if you're not careful, you can miss them. They're the spontaneous moments that happen if you let them — like jamming and singing with David Cassidy and Shirley Jones, or my solo freedom dance to "La Bamba" in a Mexican restaurant. We have to act on and give in to those moments. They don't happen often, but they're so real you can feel it. It's impossible to hold them down. All you need is encouragement; somebody to say, "Do it!" All Maureen needed was for me to say, "Come on and sing. It's Christmas." Yes! It's so simple.

But back to the manager at Chester Village: he was simply not the right person for the job. How could he be, if he was so far removed from who the residents were? He eventually retired. It was suggested we get a temporary specialty management team to come in and sort things out. They found all kinds of problems — books not balanced, unhappy staff, all sorts of bad stuff going on. Then, after a couple of false starts, they found a professional, long-term care management team and finally things started to turn around. Today it has totally changed and I am delighted to see and feel the difference in the atmosphere. It's a happy place to live.

There's only so much you can do as a volunteer but as part of the fundraising committee we helped raise a lot of money for the beautiful new building at Danforth and Warden. The Chester Village residents and staff all love the new facility. I'm really proud to have been part of that. I'm still invited to all the annual staff dinners. Without volunteers there would be no new facility.

Today, long-term care facilities are rated on residents' satisfaction and results are posted. It's a win-win situation. Long-term care facilities used to get a bad rap — not anymore. Who wouldn't enjoy choices of good meals, health care when needed, camaraderie or privacy, bowling, swimming, fitness, painting, gardening, lectures, TV, etc. It's your choice! Hooray!

CHAPTER 10

GUARDIAN ANGELS

I believe in Guardian Angels. Here are six reasons why.

1) During my teens, while I was working at Lever Brothers, my girlfriend and I used to go to Buffalo to shop every six months or so because we could buy clothes for half the price we'd pay in Toronto.

This particular night I was on my way home from one of our shopping sprees. I was alone — my girlfriend and I lived in opposite directions and we'd parted ways at the streetcar stop. We were flat broke, having spent every last cent — I couldn't even afford a taxi.

It was quite late, maybe around midnight, and very dark. I got off at my streetcar stop and started to walk down Caroline Avenue, carrying two heavy suitcases, wearing high heels (!) and totally exhausted. Suddenly I just got this very strong feeling, an instinct, that something was wrong. A car approached behind me and this feeling wouldn't leave me, but when it kept on driving I thought, Good.

I was so tired. But then the car turned around at the bottom of the street and came back up the street, and parked a little ways ahead of where I was walking. I remember thinking, Oh no, I'm too tired for this. I've got some kook following me and I just don't have time for this. For some reason, I walked right up to the car and stopped at the front bumper. Meanwhile, this guy was already out of the car, and came around to the rear door, sidewalk side. He opened the rear door, and was pretending to rummage around with something in the backseat. Thinking that I was still walking and that I would be beside the car, he leapt out, his hands up as if to grab me around the throat. When he saw me, standing two feet away, he kind of froze, startled, still with his hands in mid-air about to choke me. Thank God he wasn't towering over me because I think I would have collapsed, but he was the same height as me in heels (height can be an advantage) with a stocky build.

Somehow I managed to say, "Get back in the car or I'm going to scream." I held my bags, ordering him to get back in the car, and the image of him standing there looking like he didn't know what to do is etched in my brain. I threw him right off, because I didn't appear frightened.

I said, "Did you hear me? I said get back in the car or I'm going to scream."

He stood there staring at me like he didn't know what to do, hands still in a choking position, and I let out this piercing scream. He ran and got into the car and I said, "Now drive off or I'm going to scream again." He just sat there, so I screamed again, and finally he drove off. It occurred to me that I should get his licence number, but then I cracked. It hit me that I could have died just then, or been shoved into the back seat... What was his intention?

I somehow made it home, only ten houses away, and went in the house. My mom and dad were playing cards, waiting up for me. I tried to tell them what had just happened but I couldn't speak. It's the only time in my life when I actually lost my voice. Apparently when you get truly terrified you can't talk, and though I tried to find my voice to tell them that someone had tried to kill me out there, all I could do was gesture. My dad — a strong, strong man — leaped up but I conveyed to him through mime, No, no, he's long gone, he drove away. They gave me a shot of liquor to calm me down and then called the police. I went down to the police station the next day to see if I could identify him from the book of mug shots. Well, if I wasn't frightened before, I sure was after, looking at all these men — hundreds of them, all with criminal records! He wasn't among them.

When I think back on that episode, I'm amazed that I pulled that off. Staying calm and in control probably saved my life. You have no idea what your frame of mind is going to be when something like that happens. I don't know whether I could have done it a second time, but when I was in the middle of it, I was thinking, Oh I'm so tired, I'm carrying all these bags, I'm wearing high heels, all I want is to go home to bed, and why are you picking on me, because this is a huge inconvenience, and what do you want? Well, I know he wanted to either kill me or knock me out or something. He sure didn't want to ask me on a date!

Reflecting on this situation, I probably should not have walked on the same side of the street, and I should have taken off my shoes, dropped my bags and started running — because I can really run if motivated. But I didn't do any of those things. I'm just glad I had a Guardian Angel sitting on my shoulder.

By the way, the next day I knocked on the neighbour's door where the near-assault took place. "Did you hear anyone scream last night?"

"Oh yes," the woman said. "But I was too afraid to do anything."

Good grief. If you suspect someone's in trouble, turn on all your lights, call the police, and make lots of noise!

2) Around 1975, a man from New York arrived in Toronto and opened a model agency and school. "R" was not registered with the Ministry of Colleges and Universities, which was mandatory. I phoned the Ministry and advised the woman who was second-in-command to the director. She told me that they already knew about R, a shady character with a bad reputation, but the director of Colleges and Universities refused to close down his school. R had been notified of the regulations — he just chose to ignore the government's request.

So I said, "Well in that case leave it with me."

I typed up a letter saying, "As of this date, we, the undersigned, will no longer be paying our annual dues to the Ministry." I contacted all the schools and agencies registered with the Ministry, informing them of my intentions and they all agreed wholeheartedly. I had Marie, my secretary, take a cab around to all of them to get their signatures, then deliver the letter to the Ministry director.

Within an hour I received a phone call from the director. He said, "You cannot hold a gun to the head of the government."

My reply was, "Well I guess we'll just have to wait and see." I added, "Why are you calling me? There were ten signatures on that letter."

"I knew it was you," he ranted. "Everyone knows it was you!"

So much for presumed innocence!

Very soon, I got a call from his second-in-command. "Oh Miss Fulcher," she said in her delightful English accent, "you've never seen such excitement in your life as you've seen in the last hour around this department." Apparently the director in charge of the private schools was retiring in three months and didn't want to make waves on his watch — let the next guy deal with it. As soon as he received our document, signed by all the Toronto agents, he had a much bigger problem. He assembled all his lawyers and within hours the sheriff's office put a lock on R's door.

The next day I was in my office when my secretary buzzed and whispered, "Eleanor, the agent who was closed down is here and he's raging. What do you want me to do?" Now, I had heard some pretty bad things about this guy, but this had to be dealt with. I couldn't leave him screaming in the reception room. "Send him in," I said.

In he barges, threatening, pointing his finger at me. "You!" he shouted. "I've heard about you." (What?!)

I knew I had to do something to calm this guy down, fast. He was livid and I didn't know what he was capable of. "You know, I've actually done you a favour," I said. He looked at me a little shocked. "I know you like photography. I've seen some of your work," I said, lying through my teeth. (I'd heard he did all his own photography.)

"You have?" he said.

"Yes, and I'm wondering why you'd want to get into this business when you're such a good photographer. Your photography is where you're really going to make money — not with the agency and school."

"Do you really think so?"

And the next thing I knew, we were best friends. He sat down and took out his portfolio, showing me all these pictures, asking my advice, and I'm oohing and aahing over his photos. "Look," I said, "You can pay your fee and carry on with your agency, but I'm telling you, if you take my advice you'll be thanking me, because we could really use more talented photographers."

We shook hands and he left. The girls at the front desk were terrified for me. They'd all huddled outside my door thinking, Should we go in there and save her, or what? They couldn't believe it when they didn't hear any more screaming after a few minutes — "Is she dead?"

That was another situation when I had to think fast on my feet. When people get mad you never know what they're capable of.

3) Then there was a time when I lived on Clarendon Avenue. I finally had my own business and could afford the rent, and lived on the first floor of what is now a heritage building. I used to come home quite late from work, around 10:00 or 10:30, and would bring a couple of employees/friends back to my place for a drink and nibbles, just to end the day.

On this particular night we three girls had been sitting chatting in my living room for an hour or so. When they left I got undressed and went into the bathroom, nude, to remove my makeup. In my bedroom there was a window that didn't quite open up all the way without wiggling and jiggling it. I had complained to the superintendent and he hadn't fixed it yet.

As I was taking my makeup off in the bathroom, I heard the unmistakable sound of my bedroom window opening, or someone trying to get it open — I knew instantly that's what it was. I ran. I ran to the entrance of my apartment, banging my hip getting out the door. I made it out to the hall — but now what? My phone was on a little table in my hallway. I stood there, naked, listening and waiting and wondering if this person made it into my apartment…I didn't know. I did know I was ready to scream and I was going to run like hell if I saw him.

After what seemed like forever (probably two minutes), there was no sound, so I took a chance and crawled back into the entrance of my apartment, grabbed the phone, sat down in the hall and phoned 911. The police arrived very quickly. I heard the sirens, then heard them running down the hall so I dashed into the bathroom and grabbed a towel to wrap around me. I figured the intruder wouldn't be waiting once he heard the sirens.

The police searched the apartment and went outside to check. They told me they could see where the guy had been lying down, looking through this half-inch of space that my blinds didn't cover. They figured he'd been there quite a while watching the three of us. He'd even unscrewed the light bulb outside and unscrewed the screen on my bedroom window.

That was my Guardian Angel, call it whatever, but I am so thankful the superintendent hadn't fixed that window. If he had, the guy would have entered without my knowledge, and I would have been trapped in the bathroom! Since then, the management has installed iron bars on all the main floor windows.

4) Another time was when Bruno asked me if I'd pick up a new furnace filter from a plumbing company off Eglinton Avenue. I didn't know exactly where it was, so as I was driving I was looking up at all the signs and street names. The driver behind me got very impatient. He was honking his horn again and again even though I was waving to him to pass me. But no, he was not interested in passing me; he was interested in honking his damn horn at me. Could he not see I was looking for something?

So I did something I'd never done before and have never done since — I gave him the finger. He came up even closer. I thought, I've got to get rid of this guy, so I turned down a street, and my God, he followed me. And worse — it was a dead end! I couldn't go any farther. I was trapped. (Often, when I've tried to take a shortcut, it turns out to be a dead end.)

He drove up behind me, leapt out of his car, and I was thinking, This is it, he's going to kill me. I picked the wrong person to give the finger to. The only time in my life and I have to give it to this nutcase. I got out of the car. Eleanor: Think. Think. This guy was coming at me and he was livid. So I got out of my car and started to cry.

I looked at him all teary and said, "Ohhh, my husband's going to kill me. He told me to find this place and I can't find it and do you know where it is? I've got to find this filter..."

He couldn't understand a word I was saying because I was sobbing, and he just stood there looking at me like, Who is this nut? "Do you know what you did back there?" he yelled.

"I don't know. I was looking for this address and I can't find it and I don't know what my husband is talking about but he said to get a filter and he's going to kill me if I come home without it...Please help me." I was bawling my eyes out.

He finally gave up trying to be angry at this stupid hysterical woman, got in his car, backed up and drove off.

You really have to be on your guard. There are so many nuts out there so just do not aggravate them. Take precautions and don't think it will never happen to you, because it can.

And never, ever, give anyone the finger!

Thank you, Guardian Angel.

5) For my sixtieth birthday, I decided to have a family reunion and organized a weekend at the Spa. Relatives arrived from Winnipeg, Connecticut, New York and Toronto; there were about 50 of us. Lots of excitement, confusion, camaraderie. During the first few hours some of the kids and adults were swimming in the pool.

I was sitting at the bar having an intense conversation with my cousin Gay from New York, whom I hadn't seen in ages. Suddenly, for no reason, my eyes drifted over Gay's shoulder and I caught sight of a nose going under water. In an instant, I knew it was my beloved three-year-old grandson, Joseph. How did I know this? A nose? I ran and dived into the water (so much for my hair, makeup and new outfit!) as he sank to the bottom. I scooped him up and resurfaced and he hardly even coughed. He was fine.

Accidents like this often happen when many people are present. Everyone thinks the other person is looking after someone. Joseph simply took off his water wings and jumped into the pool — and no one had noticed. Lots of rules were put in place after that near-tragic incident. Once again my Guardian Angel was sitting on my shoulder (or my cousin's).

6) My writer/journalist friend Joan McCormick Frankel saved my life. She and I would often hang out together while working on the *Toronto Sun* Fulcher's Line columns, course curriculums or promotional flyers. (Joan is my son Marcus's godmother.) This particular time, we were up at the Spa working on a brochure, and I'd grilled some steaks for our dinner. We were sitting eating and chatting, and I swallowed a piece of steak. It went down the wrong way. It was caught in my windpipe and had cut off my breathing. I was in a total panic. It's a terrifying feeling when you can't breathe. I honestly thought I was going to die right then and there. I was frantically pointing at my throat and would you believe, Joan knew right away

Joan McCormick Frankel, who saved my life one day

what was wrong. She leapt up and stood behind me and drove her fist into my chest. The Heimlich Maneuver. She once saw it on TV and remembered the technique. It worked! The piece of meat went flying across the room and I could breathe again. If I'd been with anyone but Joan I probably wouldn't be here today. She was so knowledgeable about so many things — and this time it saved my life.

In relating this episode later to my friend Heather Jenkinson, she told me the following story. "Six of us were partying one night and drinking quite a bit and nibbling. Lots of laughing and joking around. One of the guys starts making all these crazy faces and pointing at his face. We all thought he was being funny and we all started laughing. He then collapsed on the floor and still we thought he was play-acting and continued to laugh. He died — right there on the floor in front of all of us. Something he swallowed went down the wrong way!"

I knew how close I'd come to the same scenario. Joan was my Guardian Angel.

CHAPTER 11

REFLECTIONS

Men and Women's Changing Roles

My son, Marcus, and his wife, Lori, seem to share equally in raising their two girls, Madison and Peyton, and doing housework. Both of them work, so why not? Marcus has probably changed 800 diapers, unlike my husband who never changed a diaper in his life. Well, he did once, and that was once too often. When Angela was one year old, I left her with Bruno for an hour and she pooped in her diapers. So instead of actually changing her diaper, he took her up to my bathtub, ran the water, and held her bum — with the diaper still on — under the tap. When I got home I went upstairs and saw this dirty diaper in my bathtub and my daughter running around nude. I said, "What is this?"

He said, "Well, she pooped."

I said, "Yes. So you clean her and put on a fresh diaper."

"Well, I did clean her. I rinsed her off."

"Then you put on a fresh diaper."

"Well, I didn't know where the diapers were." I am not exaggerating.

My friend Cathy has one better. She told me that she once left her daughter with her husband for a few hours, and came back to find her wearing not one, not two, but three diapers. He thought all you had to do was put another diaper on top of a dirty one. Men of that generation were that bad.

There were male jobs and female jobs. My dad had a name for every task: "that's women's work"; "that's men's work." My husband is almost as bad. Now he sees Marcus doing all this domestic stuff and doesn't know what to think. Marcus is now the president of Bruno's company, but he's not a slave to it. He likes cooking, playing with the kids, going boating with them, taking them places, shopping — he shares responsibilities. Bruno gets annoyed sometimes if Marcus has to leave the office in the middle of their discussion to pick up the kids or shop or whatever. I say, "That's the way it is today. They share."

It's a totally different world, and the Marcuses of this world are wonderful. I never would have thought my son would be changing diapers, cooking great meals, cleaning up and sharing duties. I'm so proud of him.

I think we've come a long way. Men of our era didn't share those responsibilities. It would have been considered sissy stuff. Many of them were workaholics — some of them still are. They were all business. Business was number one — then family. They were the breadwinners. That was their job. No more was expected of them. It's not that way anymore, and I'm happy to see that change.

Even so, women still have the biggest juggling act and that may never change. A lot more men have to step up to the plate and contribute more. They have to stop with this macho thing; they have to get past that because it's not helpful and everyone can see through it today. We women today admire men who share responsibilities and who are handy around the house.

Women of a Certain Age

I was talking recently to Joan Egan, my former Spa director, and she told me we had to do something to change the image of women over 70. "Everyone thinks we're decrepit," she said. I agreed.

My girlfriends, most of them over 70, are all still attractive, chic and very busy. We pass our energy to one another. It's so important to have good friends and I cherish all of mine. First there's the Bridge Group that meets once a week for lunch and bridge, plus once in a while for duplicate. Second is the Dinner and Theatre Group; we meet at least once a month. The RCYC girls got together regularly for many years. Then there's the travel group, called the Crazy Eights — an annual cruise group — and "The Girls," who have been getting together two or three times a year since we were teen-

The Girls, 2012

Crazy Eights, 2006

The Globetrotters at the Lambton Country Club, 1979

agers. We all lead very active lives. Sure we all have a few health problems — some major, some minor — but that doesn't stop us.

My grandmother, Tella Fulcher, was old at 50. She would wear a housedress, no makeup, and gray hair in a bun. Women back then seemed to start looking "old" a lot earlier. It undoubtedly had everything to do with their hard lives and being always in the house as

The RCYC (Royal Canadian Yacht Club) Girls

wives and mothers of large families with little help. God bless them. Today, women have choices. We are so lucky.

Women over 65 can look terrific if they so choose. Beauty is a habit. You get into looking good for yourself, because it makes you feel better and it motivates you.

Attitude is everything. In Europe, they tend to revere older women more than we do in North America. Is that because of Hollywood, I wonder, where youth is everything? In Europe, "women of a certain age" are admired for their charm, chic and wisdom. Let's hope more North American women develop a stronger sense of individuality and self-esteem and learn to enjoy their prime and wear their years with grace and pride — "character" lines and all. With a new awareness of fitness and increased energy through nutrition and exercise, women of any age can keep a lot of people guessing about the number of candles on their birthday cakes. Chances are, they could care less about who's counting. Age is just a number. Some people are "old" at 40 — some are "young" at 80.

I gave many talks to seniors' groups, and the one thing I always stressed was there is joy in aging if you know that what counts is what's inside. The beauty of the soul shines through in the beauty of the face. Laugh lines look better than scowl lines as we age. So laugh a lot.

Fashion Versus Style

When I was a young woman in my late teens and early twenties, it was just accepted that we'd force our bodies into waist cinchers and girdles so tight that we could hardly breathe or walk. I had a waist cincher that was 5 inches by 5 inches. It took me forever to get into that thing but it gave me the desired result — a waist about 18 inches. Then you have the crinolines billowing out from your beautiful little teeny weeny waistline and you'd look just like a little dream girl. I can't believe I wore those items — all day! I don't know how many girdles I had — and I weighed 117 pounds! The girdle was meant to eliminate all suggestion of actually having a bum. I remember following one of our teachers up some stairs and playfully whacking her on the rear end to get her to hurry up. It was obvious she wasn't wearing a girdle and I was shocked! I said, "Doris, you don't wear a girdle?"

She said, "Shhhh. No, I've never worn one. Don't tell anyone, okay?"

I've never forgotten that incident because it was symbolic of the times. Women were brainwashed into thinking that if they didn't wear girdles or waist cinchers or high heels they were not feminine, that there was something wrong with them, that men would not find them attractive. I fell for this intimidation like everybody else. Also, I used to shop for hours in high heels, suffering all the while. Why?

It irritates me to think of what we went through. I've rebelled to the other extreme now because I refuse to wear high heels. I wear one-inch heels if we're going out on a formal occasion, but that's it. Whenever they try to bring back foolish fashions, I think, Rebel! You can look smart and be comfortable. They are not at odds. Find the image you're comfortable with and stick to it. Make your own statement.

The other day, I was driving up around Branksome Hall, a private girls' school, with my daughter, Angela, and happened to be there when the graduating class was crossing Mt. Pleasant Road. All these young girls were walking so awkwardly, some of them almost hobbling, and I wondered what was wrong with them. Then I leaned forward and saw their feet and I had my answer. All these girls were wearing platform shoes that were so high they could hardly walk. They were bent over trying to keep their balance and concentrating on not falling flat on their faces. How attractive is that? It's not, but that's how ingrained fashion is. Nothing's changed. Girls still think they have to wear these ridiculously uncomfortable shoes in order to be in fashion.

And false eyelashes! They used to be so heavy your eyes would almost be closing at the end of the day. I remember taking them off at night and feeling oh-my-God, such relief — it was almost like taking off a girdle. But they were "in fashion."

Fashion is fun but don't be a slave to it. Adapt fashion to your own taste and find your own style.

The Mirror Image

Very few people are natural beauties. It's what you do with what you have that matters. We all have things about our faces or bodies we would change if given a choice.

Women are especially hard on themselves. Even movie stars are self-conscious about their "flaws." Frank Rasky, with whom I collaborated on a book, *Models and Movie Stars* (we never actually finished writing it), told me that Raquel Welch told him she was painfully aware of her big legs. Marilyn Monroe hated the red veins in her nose. Rita Hayworth, Kim Novak and Yvonne de Carlo, all reigning sex queens in their day, confided to Frank their concern about their big hips. Liza Minnelli told him she always felt her big eyes made her look like a cartoon character. And on and on.

I was born with a slight imperfection of my right ear — it was a little more pointed than rounded — and it didn't affect anything except that as a teenager I was self-conscious about it. I couldn't wear my hair pulled back because it stuck out a little. One day I told my mother I didn't like my ear and she said, "Oh, when you were born the doctor said that he could fix it with a little nip and tuck, but I told him no."

Hello? "Why not?" I asked incredulously.

"Oh," she said, "you're a girl; it won't show."

I've never forgotten her saying that because my ear really, really bothered me.

Years passed, and one day I was getting my hair done at Gus Caruso's. Dear Gus. He's gone now but he was the absolute best. "Eleanor," he said, "why don't you get this ear pulled back? There are so many more hairstyles you could wear." He said he knew a doctor who had performed this ear operation for a well-known singer client of his, and gave me the doctor's name.

When I went to see this doctor, he hardly even looked at my ear but said, "Oh yeah, sure, that's easily done. And while we're at it, you've got a little bit of a bump on your nose. We can take care of that too." It hadn't really occurred to me to do anything to my nose, but when he said, "You're in the beauty field and you must have a lot of people coming and going whom you could refer. Why don't I just fix it for you. I'll do it no charge." Well, okay, two-for-one — what a deal! It sounded like a simple procedure, so I agreed. I told the staff at Thornton's, where I was the Associate Director, that I'd be off for a few days, thinking I'd be back to work in a week.

After the surgery, I came out of the operating room looking like I'd been hit by a train. I was completely black and blue, head all wrapped up, two eyes peering out of the bandages. My mother came to visit and fainted when she saw me. I looked in the mirror and said to myself, Well, that's it. My beauty days are over! I berated myself for being so stupid to allow myself to be talked into a totally unnecessary operation. I phoned Gary Carter and told him it was going to be a while before I could come back to work. But what I could do during this time off was rewrite the school curriculum, which I'd been trying to get at for years. So that's what I proceeded to do. Well, I thought, this is it. I'll become a writer. A recluse. Then no one will see me. I had already reinvented myself.

Then my face started to heal, the bandages came off, and I actually started to look normal again! My ear was just as flat as could be. I cried because it was so beautiful.

After a couple of weeks I went back to the doctor for my checkup. "All right," he said, "let's get those stitches out." Stitches? I didn't know there were stitches. As he took the stitches out, I could feel the ear coming back out. I was devastated. My nose didn't look all that different and my ear was not only not flat, it was kind of squared off, not even a nice round shape.

I said, "What did you do?"

He looked at it and said, "Oh yes…I guess I should have…" and proceeded to get very technical. "You'll have to come back and we'll redo it."

Redo it? I told him to forget it. I wasn't going to go back to this doctor who hadn't even really examined the ear in the first place and put me through all that for nothing. I had trusted him and he messed up. Back then, cosmetic surgery wasn't nearly as common as it is now. If I had it to do over again, I would never have done it.

Today I wear my hair back and no one even notices my ear, no one except me. We are usually our own worst critics. You can think something's wrong with you but it's really so minor it's not even worth thinking about.

After I sold my business, I remember thinking, Oh good — now I don't have to wear any makeup. Well — that thought lasted one day. I couldn't stand looking at myself. I then understood that I like to look good for me. I have more energy and motivation. I even *think* better when I look good.

My morning routine hasn't changed much. I'm up at 6:20 a.m., exercise for half an hour, shower, set my hair, do my makeup, do the crossword puzzle, the bridge column, read the paper, get dressed, eat breakfast, etc. All of that takes two hours in total and that's it for the day. By 9:30 a.m. I'm ready for anything! If I'm going out for lunch or dinner I do a touch up for five minutes, and maybe change jewelry or jackets, and voila! If someone calls and asks me if I'm available for such and such, I don't have to stop and think about what I'd have to do to get ready. I love knowing that I don't have to think about my appearance again. I get on with my day, knowing that I'm looking okay. I do it Monday to Friday. Saturday and Sunday I'm a little more flexible.

I'm not a good traveller. Good female travellers are often women who don't wear much makeup, who can wear one outfit for ten days by just washing it out every few days. They pull their hair back in a ponytail and that's it — they're gone. I couldn't do that in a million years. I've got to have my stuff with me. My husband can be ready in five minutes. He comes home from the office, throws a few things into a bag and he's off to Europe. That's not me. I'm not comfortable travelling unless I have my makeup, rollers, shampoo, etc. — my stuff. Men don't seem to worry. They go into a hotel and use the shampoo that's in the bathroom. Sometimes there's even a razor supplied. In my next life I'll be a man because it's much easier.

Once when we were going to Europe with Marcus and Lori, my husband announced that everyone would be allowed just one medium piece of luggage in order to fit everything in one car once we arrived. Well, a big argument ensued because I needed a bigger bag. To my amazement, Marcus said, "Oh Dad, let her take her stuff. We'll manage." He understood. Thank you, Marcus.

First Impressions Still Count

It's a fact that people make snap judgments based on appearance. Case in point: when Susan Boyle, that frumpish woman from a tiny town in Scotland, sang on *Britain's Got Talent*. I loved watching how the audience and judges first reacted, expecting a disaster out of this dowdy woman in her mid-forties. There was a lot of eye rolling — until she started to sing a song from *Les Misérables*. She has an incredible voice. The judges and audience were amazed. There was hardly a dry eye! She had never had the opportunity before this show. She'd been limited to small pubs in her village. But now she was on her way to stardom.

Appearances do count. The most successful people in business are those who have the complete package — talent, brains, drive and, yes, image. They walk with confidence and speak with confidence and they are well groomed. Personal grooming will never go out of style, and it says a lot about the person. It advertises self-esteem, or a lack of it. Nails are clean and shaped, hair is shiny and brushed, clothes are neat and fit well. Yes, it takes time and care to get your act together, but it pays big dividends. Well-groomed people look as if they're in charge of their life, and they appear to be organized and self-confident.

If I see someone walk on stage or stand up to give a speech and they're all slouched over with dreadful posture and rumpled clothes, right away I've got a negative impression of them. I find it a bit of an insult when people haven't bothered or cared enough to dress smartly and carry themselves well. It may be subconscious but we can't help but form impressions based on what a person looks like. That person giving the speech might then open his or her mouth and be absolutely captivating. By then you are past the visual. But why not have it all?

In the real world, business is all about relating to people and you have to always put your best foot forward. If you look in the mirror and like what you see — if you say, "Yes, that's the message I'm trying to get across, that's the image I'd like to project" — that's good. I'm not saying you should go so far as to be vain or narcissistic about it — "Hey, look at me. Aren't I great?" — but do the best you can to look good.

I think this is especially important for women in power — and looking good does not mean looking sexy. Look at *The Globe and Mail's* photos of newly appointed CEOs or top managers and you can see that 80 percent of the women have their act together with their overall image. They do not show a lot of cleavage nor do they wear skirts that barely cover their behinds. This is something that young women have to understand. If they want to be taken seriously, they can't go around with bare midriffs and exposed cleavage.

But look at their role models. I'm annoyed when these TV shows really play up a woman's breasts. You watch any of the *CSI*-type shows where women are supposed to be competent police officers, and they're exposing cleavage. Can't they be just smart ladies without showing all that skin? Whoever produces these shows feels this is necessary in order to grab men's attention. How sad is that? If the storyline is so weak that you need cleavage to sell it, no one's going to watch it anyway.

I even see it in the morning when I watch the news channel. Every day the female newscaster is wearing a different outfit. She's wearing a strapless dress, or an off-the-shoulder top with long hair tumbling down and full evening makeup — eye shadow, eyeliner, false lashes, the works. She's doing the 7 a.m. news but she's dressed for dinner and dancing! Her appearance actually detracts from her delivery of the news.

Whoever is advising these women is greatly mistaken. Women, especially those in the public eye, must find their own image and their own voice, not those created by producers, makeup artists and hair stylists. Yes, be open to suggestions, but you have the final say.

Grace, Poise, Decency and Manners

I think it's sad that the Eleanor Fulcher self-improvement type of training is not a priority today. I know it would help a lot of young people. How do they build confidence in schools? Do they put you on a stage in front of an audience? Do they put you in front of a mic as emcee? Do they advise you on your best colours, wardrobe, makeup, hair, social graces, personality tips? No. Who wouldn't benefit from this input? Yes, in time you may discover the best you, but how long will it take? Years. With proper training you could do it in a few weeks.

It's coming back, though. I noticed recently that the Massachusetts Institute of Technology offers lessons on charm, poise and social graces. They realize that it's not just academic and technical skills that are going to contribute to a student's success. They're acknowledging that if you don't have the visuals, it's ten times harder out there in the real world. There are many companies now offering courses on etiquette, such as using the right cutlery, and public speaking. If you have the brain power and the image, personality, social graces and so on, well, you've got a winner. In the competitive marketplace today, make sure you've got it all.

And where has common decency gone? I saw a film clip on television recently that really made me very sad, about a two-year-old child who had wandered into traffic on a busy street in a Chinese city and had been hit by a car. And no one, no one, went to help this little girl lying there. The reporter said, "China has lost its soul."

I feel the same way about Canada sometimes. I read a letter in the newspaper from a handicapped woman who was forced to sit on the floor of a subway train when no one would get up and give her their seat. What does that say about society today? Where are our manners? Where is our soul?

In our course curriculum, we had a class called Social Graces and Etiquette, where this sort of social situation would come up in discussion. It's about caring about others and showing manners. Today, I try to pass along to my grandchildren what that means. I recently was babysitting my grandchildren Madison and Peyton and took the opportunity to share an article I'd cut out of the newspaper about children and manners. (I couldn't have just handed it to Marcus and Lori because they might think I was criticizing their parenting — I wasn't — and I couldn't hand it to the kids because they'd think I was criticizing their manners.) It was about a little Parisienne girl who visited a Canadian family and inadvertently taught the kids how to be polite — everything was Madame this and Madame that. "Madame, do you mind if I can't quite finish eating this?" I was alone with Madison and said to her, "Oh Madison, I don't want to get up and get my glasses. Could you just read this to me?" and gave her the article. She read it beautifully (she's ten), asking me about one or two words she didn't understand — which gave me a chance to open the discussion further. We talked about manners generally. I think it's important that children learn these things and be considerate of other people. You have to teach that — it's not always something that comes naturally. Children learn by example — and many examples out there today are not desirable.

When I was young, my brother and I had our specific chores to help out around the house. Everybody was part of the dinner hour — I set the table, Fred did the dishes. Dinner didn't just appear magically. It was expected of you to help out almost from the time you could walk. When the grandchildren are here with me, I'll say, "You're a big girl now. Could you carry this to the table?" Or, "Could you help me set the table?" And they like it; they feel grown up and trusted and it builds their self-respect — and respect for others.

It used to be automatic to get up and give an elderly person a seat on the streetcar or bus. When did that change, and why? I think it's because kids today are more pampered. They don't have to do things like that. It would be a big stretch for them because they haven't been in the habit. If all your life you've been expected to make your bed, to get dressed, tidy your room, and be involved in the household, it becomes second nature.

Schools today don't teach manners. Students are allowed to call their teachers Barb or Joan or Ed or Ted or whatever. Teachers can't even pat someone on the back for doing a good job for fear of being sued. Their authority is being taken away from them and kids are taking advantage. Students have to be taught respect for authority, rules, for our government, and for their elders. I do not like an 18-year-old waiter calling me Eleanor after he's read my name on my credit card. It's disrespectful. Call me Ms. Arnold if you don't know whether I'm married.

Once when Bruno and I were visiting in Switzerland, he suddenly locked arms with our host, whom he'd known for many years, and they toasted each other. I said, "What was that about?" Bruno said, "He just gave me permission to call him by his first name." They'd gone past the acquaintance stage; it's a passage. I was stunned. But that's their culture, and it's nice. It's respectful. Where did that go? This casual attitude has gone too far.

Some time ago, businesses brought in "casual Fridays" but they have largely stopped that because employees would come in wearing jeans and T-shirts. I invited someone to dinner once and told him it was casual, meaning he needn't bother with a tie, and he arrived at my door in a hockey shirt! Now we have the term "dressy casual" — meaning not jeans and T-shirts. To me, that term just means no tie.

Whenever I hear someone say, "Oh, I could never go out on a stage or stand up at a sales meeting," I think, Oh yes you could. But confidence doesn't just happen. You have to be taught certain things, and you have to earn it and develop it.

Yes, overall self-improvement education is due — overdue — for a comeback. I look at fashion today and I think the women are really confused. A lot of them don't know where to go with their image and they're buying crazy things. Nothing's coordinated; it's as if they've just thrown it on and hoped for the best. But if you go into the business world, it's important to have a certain look.

I have a lot of opinions that don't matter anymore because I'm not in the business world, but if I were to go out today and lecture to a company's employees, my message would be to get a look and get it together and save yourself a lot of money.

If you're a businesswoman, get your "uniform" together, like men do. Keep it simple and stylish and choose clothes and accessories that are appropriate, easy to coordinate, and that you can put on quickly and efficiently. Don't be dictated to by the fashion designers, because they tend to take over your wardrobe.

I decided long ago that I had a summer look and a winter look. In winter, I have black as my basic colour — black pants, black turtle-necks, black short sleeve tops and black long sleeve tops — and then

I just change my jacket or cardigan or vest, which can be any colour, and my jewelry. I go a little more dramatic with my makeup in the evening if we're going out.

In summer, I wear a lot of beige. If I'm going out I can just change my top, maybe add some jewelry, and I'm ready. When I was younger I tried all kinds of hairstyles. It was fun. I wasn't ready to settle into one look. Besides, my industry was all about change.

My former hairdresser, John Steinberg, used to always tell me, "We've got to find a look for you and keep it forever."

I said, "I get so bored. I like change." I'd bring in pictures and tell him, "Here. Here's the look I want." It didn't matter if it was better or worse; it was just different. Now I wear my hair in a certain simple style almost always, because I want something easy that I don't have to fiddle around with every day. I visit my fabulous hairdresser, Brien, every six weeks for a cut and colour — for ten years. That's it.

It's what you feel comfortable with. It's the same with interior decorating. You have to go with something that is you. When we were decorating the interior of the Spa, we started out with an interior decorator from Montreal. I told her what I felt I would like to have — all earth colours, because it was so restful in Muskoka, with the water and the trees and the sunsets. But she was a blue person and came in with all these ideas that were so contrary to what I wanted. She wasn't even listening to what I was saying.

I had to let her go and I ended up doing almost all the interior decorating myself. I wanted it simple, with a feeling of homeyness and comfort. You don't have to be an interior decorator to know what you like. Sometimes it's enough to know what you don't like. To this day everyone loves the simple, relaxing décor and atmosphere of the Spa. Go with your instincts.

CHAPTER 12

LIFE LESSONS

The Show Must Go On

I live by principles that life has taught me, and something that I've carried with me forever — or at least since the time I broke the bone in my foot but still performed — is that you can get through just about anything.

Our Model of the Year shows would often have 400 men, women and children graduating, so chances are that at some point one of them would come to me and say, "Eleanor, I'm not feeling well. I can't do it; I can't go on…" I'd tell them the story about breaking my foot, then say, "You know what? I don't want to hear it. You're doing the show. You'll get through it, because this is showbiz and we're going to see what you're made of. If you don't, you can just write yourself off as far as this field is concerned. Supposing you're booked for a shoot, with thousands of dollars at stake and people waiting for you, and you wake up and you don't feel well. No one wants to hear about it! In other words, are you made of the right stuff? That's what we've got to find out." I wouldn't listen to them or pamper them. I just said, "No, that's not good enough." When you've been through it yourself and you realize you can get through just about anything, it teaches you to be really strong.

I think life is in many ways similar to show business. The show must go on. No whining, no excuses, no "poor me." Just do it.

It's the Thought that Counts

I loved my Grade 3 teacher, Miss Beal. I remember saying to my classmates that we had to get her something for her birthday. I collected about two cents from all her students and bought Miss Beal a hanky on behalf of all of us. A hanky. Well, she was so moved by this little gift, this pretty lace hanky from all her students, that she cried. She must have known that no one had any money.

Ever since then, I've known that it's the thought that counts — it has nothing to do with the price of the gift. Like my grandmother Tella buying me the apple or the chocolate éclair — it meant so much to me. People shouldn't think that you have to have a lot of money to do something meaningful. A card with a nice handwritten note is all that is needed. The thought — the good intention. That can mean everything to the recipient.

I send many special occasion cards every month. There are a lot of people that I can't get to see for one reason or another, but what I can do is send a card. I buy a lot of funny cards, as I like to visualize them laughing. I have a big box I keep filled with cards for birthdays and special events. Every month I look at my book of who's having a special occasion. It doesn't take me more than half an hour once a month. It's just to say I'm thinking of you, I miss you, love you, whatever. They might be in Switzerland or New York or Winnipeg and you might not see them for years, but you can keep the connection and let them know you're thinking about them and that you feel your relationship is special. I know it means something to them because many of them reciprocate. I love receiving written notes or cards and often reread them many times.

Sometimes you don't know how much a card or a gesture or a phone call can mean to someone who really needs it. An example is a dear friend of mine, "L," who was separated from her husband and raising three young children on her own. She had a very tough time of it for about ten years. She was juggling work, babysitters, household duties, cooking — one can hardly imagine the stress. (She's since met a wonderful, highly successful guy.) I'd always make sure I remembered her children on their birthdays and Christmas. I'd call her just to chat and remind her how amazing she was and occasionally I'd treat her to lunch. I always felt I should do much more but we lived so far apart and our lives were so busy, it's all we could both manage.

At our Christmas Open House that Bruno and I host every year, L bumped into a former close friend (when L was still with her husband). As is often the case when couples break up, friends choose sides. This former friend looked at L in amazement and said, "You and Eleanor have kept in touch all these years?" Well, L went into this long story about me — it was like a eulogy. It was such a loving tribute — about how I was the only one who had kept in touch with her and the kids and how I'd always been there for her and supported her when she was down, and on and on and on. I was practically in tears it was so beautiful. And here I'd been feeling guilty all these years because I didn't think I'd done enough.

The lesson I learned was just pick up the phone if you have a friend in need. A phone call and card can mean so much.

By the way, we recently had lunch and just as I reached for the cheque, she beat me to it. With a twinkle in her eyes and a smile she said, "It's okay, Eleanor, I can afford it now." After ten years of struggle her life is like a fairy tale come true. Her children are doing well and she's found true love. She never gave up. No one deserves happiness more than she does. And there's more. L had been working at this large company for years while raising her three children. The president of the company had declared the "no dating" policy years before. One can only imagine his confusion when he sees L day after day and is obviously very attracted to her, but — his rules, his policy — hands off. Then L gets breast cancer and is in the hospital for treatment. And who comes to visit her with flowers and affection? Right. Anyway, she fully recovers, hands in her notice (at his request) and they've been together ever since. Who needs Hollywood!

Confidence Grows Step By Step

All the things that happen to you in life bring you to where you are. Everything that happens to you in life teaches you a lesson, if you're willing to learn. The incident with Miss Kennedy, my Grade 7 teacher who destroyed my confidence, stayed with me for a long, long time. From this experience I was able to understand fear of public speaking and empathize and help others overcome this problem. If someone came in to the school or agency and said, "I will never, ever get up in front of an audience," I was determined that yes, they would. I developed a program that made it easy for them to do it in little steps — not big steps, little steps, like Mr. Whitley did for me. I'd throw something at them at the last minute, maybe to just stand up and say their name and introduce someone. It was designed to build confidence in small but important ways. "Oh, Linda, you know how to do that; I've seen you do that really well. Would you mind teaching Sally how to do it?" How wonderful to be told that you're actually good enough to teach somebody else!

But I had a secret for many years. Even at Thornton's, although I was good at teaching others, deep down I was afraid that that feeling I had in Grade 7 would return unexpectedly — that right in the middle of something I wouldn't be able to speak. I'd just freeze. I became good at allocating and delegating so I didn't have to get up and actually do it, because I still had that fear right up until I left Thornton's and started my own business. Then, I had no choice. I couldn't hand it to someone else and say here, you're good at public speaking, you do this one, and you do the show and you do this. No one ever guessed. They just thought I was wonderful to give them all these chances.

One of the first public speaking jobs with my own business was when I was working with George Abbott, the top makeup artist in Canada, who hated public speaking. "Eleanor," he said, "don't ask me to speak. I'll do anything with makeup, but do not ask me to speak." He'd made it very clear, so that was fine — I had to be the spokesperson. It eventually became easy, but you have to have the opportunity to do it over and over; you can't just do it once or twice. In my business, the students had free practice classes every night from 5 o'clock to 6 o'clock. I assigned a teacher to supervise, and I'd have a mic set up on the stage. Every night each student would stand up at the mic and announce their name and introduce the next student. And so it went until everyone had a chance at the mic saying one brief introduction. Next, we'd add a line — maybe where you were from. Every night we did this, and they became more and more comfortable. Some of these students had never been in front of an audience, so I made sure they had lots of opportunities. Next thing I know they were all public speakers. They were all volunteering! You can't really succeed in business if you're not prepared to conduct a meeting or speak in front of people, so I felt this was a very important part of the course curriculum. Just knowing you can do it if you have to do it gives you so much more confidence.

Once, a man and his wife came to the school for help. He was a rising star in business and needed his wife beside him at all these social events, but this gal was so shy and lacking in self-confidence that it was becoming a real problem. I told them she would have to come in every night and practise. "Oh that's fine. No problem."

This girl was beautiful, and it didn't take her long to become very comfortable on the runway. In fact, she eventually became one of our top models. And the kicker is that she left her husband. She had found herself and didn't like who she had been. So she left. I'm not sure that's what her husband had in mind when he brought her in! I've seen this same scenario many times. A man wants a young, beautiful girl to idolize and worship him. But sometimes he does not want her to grow up.

The training program really transformed many lives. That's what I loved about it. All kinds of people benefitted from a few weeks of our classes. It didn't matter how educated they were, how rich they were — people often suffer from the same insecurities. Young girls today might look like they have all the confidence in the world, but it's often false confidence. Ask them to get up in front of a group and talk about any subject they like, and most would not feel comfortable. You have to be exposed to this type of situation often and regularly, until it becomes second nature.

I was reading *Outliers* the other day, and it said everyone has potential at something but it's what you do with it that makes all the difference in your life. Take Bill Gates. Do you think Bill Gates is smarter than everyone else? No. Was he a computer wiz as a kid? Yes. When Bill Gates went to school, the computer was really new, and everyone was entitled to three hours or so of computer practice a week, but because Bill Gates' parents were well off, they negotiated with the school to donate a certain amount if he could have 30 hours at the computer, not three hours. Yes, he had advantages and opportunity, but look what he did with it. Not every kid who might have had that opportunity would have transformed it into what Bill Gates did. When I read that, I thought, Good for him. He earned it.

It's what you do with opportunity when it knocks. You've got to open that door and run through. It may never come again. I've seen potentially great models blow fabulous opportunities because it wasn't a convenient time or whatever — thinking the opportunity would come again. But it might not. Years later, after agents and clients dropped them, they would voice their regrets at missed opportunities. Be determined. Be steadfast. Be ready.

CHAPTER 13

FINDING MR. RIGHT

Claustrophobia is the fear of being enclosed, trapped in a small space. For me, it meant losing control of my life. I developed claustrophobia when I was 24.

I was once engaged to a wonderful man. He was clever, charming and handsome. But I knew something wasn't right. Despite my reservations, we went ahead with marriage plans. We set a date, sent out wedding invitations, presents started coming in — and then we started looking for an apartment. After looking at several, we found one in Rosedale that we liked very much. When I did a walk around, I had the strangest feeling that the walls were closing in on me. I told my fiancé that I thought the rooms were very small. "What do you mean?" he said. "This is the largest apartment we've seen." (I know now that it was indeed a huge apartment.) But he signed the lease, paid the deposit, and that was going to be our new home, one month from that day.

That night, I woke up drenched in sweat, having had a terrible nightmare. I bolted upright in bed and thought, What am I doing?

Early in the morning, I phoned my fiancé at his office. "Put a stop payment on the cheque," I said, and hung up. I knew that if I stayed on the phone he'd talk me out of it; he was a very persuasive person. I felt I had no choice but to back out. He had cast me in the role of the housewife with the white picket fence, with 2.5 kids, and even though I was working at Thornton's at the time, that's exactly the future I would have had. He was certainly able to support me and the house and children. He deserved — and wanted — that kind of woman. That wasn't me.

We did call off the wedding. What a mess I'd made of things. Gifts arriving. Out-of-town guests booked. Wedding arrangements made. It would have been much easier to go through with it and I really thought I could, but suddenly my future loomed before me and it wasn't what I wanted. I would have felt totally trapped in that marriage, just like I would have felt trapped in the typing pool at Lever Brothers.

To this day I have claustrophobia, especially in airplanes, small spaces and elevators. I eventually went to a psychiatrist who specialized in claustrophobia. As part of the treatment he would take me into an elevator and make me go up one floor by myself, then he'd meet me, and I'd go to another floor, and so on.

After ten weeks he thought I was cured. So the next day, I had a hair appointment on the third floor of a building. I went into the elevator by myself, anxious to prove I could do it. But to my disappointment a young woman ran to the elevator doors as they were closing and pushed them open. She must have thrown the automatic mechanism off. The doors closed, but the elevator didn't move.

I began to talk to myself. Okay, just do what the psychiatrist told you. Stay calm. Put your mind elsewhere. All this time this lady was pressing buttons and mumbling. "We seem to be stuck." All of a sudden I went nuts. I started banging on the door, "Help! Let me out of here!" I just lost it.

This lovely young lady took my arm and said, "It's all right, it's all right. We're going to be fine." Suddenly the elevator started moving. It went up, past the third floor (my floor), right to the top, where the doors opened. I leapt out and headed for the stairs. There was no way I was getting in another elevator! But the staircase was closed — under repairs with scaffolding, drop sheets, the works. Help! Is this a conspiracy or something? The day after I graduated from claustrophobia school!

"Okay," said the woman. "We'll take the other elevator. Come with me; it's all right." She took me firmly by the arm, now fully in charge, and somehow got me down to the third floor. We had appointments with the same hairdresser.

I told her my story about being claustrophobic.

"Oh my gosh, you poor dear. You'll be okay," she said. "Sorry I have to go now — I'm getting married in two hours! I'm just on my way to get my hair done."

Now, if anyone should have been going nuts it was her, getting married in two hours! But she was so calm and I was a wreck. I'm sure she's told her children the story about her run-in with a maniac on the elevator on her wedding day.

I still have claustrophobia, but I can deal with it as long as someone's with me in an elevator. But this fear of being enclosed in small spaces was about something much larger — my fear of being trapped in life, playing a role that I couldn't control. And that was the message: I don't like situations where I have no control, like elevators or planes.

Serendipity: Meeting Bruno

When I was in my twenties, it was mainly through friends that single women met single men. A friend would know somebody and set you up and the four of you would go out for drinks or dinner or whatever. These days it's all e-mail and texting and online dating sites. It seems to me it was somewhat more personal and romantic back then.

Anyway, Betty-Jean Talbot-Hoffman, a friend of mine whom I mentioned earlier, told me her husband, Nolan, knew a man they thought I'd like. His name was Bruno Arnold. Sure, I said, why not?

At this time, Betty-Jean was on the CBC program *701* and she was scheduled to do a live interview at George's Spaghetti House that night. Nolan was supposed to call Bruno and tell him where we were meeting for dinner, but he lost Bruno's number! He couldn't even remember where he worked. I said, "Never mind. I'll call a friend and he'll join us." I called a friend of mine and asked him if he'd like to go to dinner with me and two friends, and he agreed.

So the four of us are in George's having dinner, when Nolan suddenly looks up and whispers to me, "You won't believe this, but that's Bruno Arnold over there." And there was Bruno, sitting alone at a table. He hadn't known we were going to George's and had waited and waited for Nolan's call. He finally gave up and went out to dinner by himself. With all the restaurants in Toronto, what were the chances Bruno would end up a few tables away from us?

Nolan went over and apologized and invited Bruno to join us for dinner, but Bruno declined. However, he did come over long enough to say hello and meet us. (Of course, my date had no idea he was a stand-in for this guy standing at our table!) There is no way Bruno and I would have connected after that because he was so ticked off with Nolan.

Hoping to make up for his gaffe, Nolan called Bruno and me and invited us to a party at their house in Hamilton. So Bruno and I hooked up for dinner before we drove to the party. We went to the Franz Joseph Room at the Walker House Hotel on Front Street in Toronto. We ended up talking, talking, and talking, drinking wine and enjoying each other's company, and decided to pass on the party. Who wants to drive to Hamilton anyway? So that's how we met. Is that not serendipity?

We started dating, became engaged about a year later, and were married October 6, 1962. BJ was my maid of honour and Nolan was an usher.

My Wedding and Honeymoon

I can't tell the story of my wedding without telling the story of the night before. It all started months prior to my wedding day, when Pierre Berton invited me to be a guest on his television show as the featured "bachelorette." It was a term that had just been coined, a much nicer label than "old maid," which is what over-25 and single ladies were called back then. Pierre's program was to be about single men and women talking about their lifestyles. The requirements were that you had to be single, run your own business, have your own apartment, and have an active social life. I qualified as I was quite happily single, had just started my own business, I was living in a nice apartment, and dating. There were supposed to be three women and three men on the show, but apparently they could not find one other bachelorette who fit these qualifications. So there was just me and three bachelors. I knew two of the men. One, Don Fontana, was a tennis pro and one was a businessman. The other was an actor, Reg, a real self-centred egotist.

As soon as the cameras starting rolling, Reg looked at me and said, "So Eleanor, how many men have you slept with?" The year was 1962. This was a shocking question at the time (now it's just rude). Needless to say, all hell broke loose.

Well, Don Fontana leapt to his feet, ready to take this guy on, and shouted, "How dare you talk to Eleanor like that?"

Pierre Berton was trying to calm things down. "Now Reg, that's enough of that. We can't have that kind of thing…"

I was so rattled, all I could think was, Get me out of here! After a few minutes Pierre asked Reg to leave the show because he wouldn't shut up. He just wanted publicity for being outrageous. I don't remember the rest of the show, I was so upset. In those days your sex life was not something you talked about, let alone on television! To add to it, I was recently engaged to Bruno. I had discussed my engagement with Pierre, wishing to bow out of the show, but he said since I was still officially "single" it was fine that I appear on the show.

After the show was taped, Pierre called and said, "Eleanor, tell me again when you're getting married."

"October 6," I said.

"Good. We're airing the show on October 5!"

The night before I was getting married, I sat up and watched the show. I hadn't told anyone about it, not even Bruno — especially not Bruno. They showed the entire segment — no editing. I was devastated. What if Bruno saw it? Or some wedding guests? I finally went to bed, a wreck. I woke up with a dreadful cold the next morning — my wedding day!

I was sniffing and coughing and totally miserable. I thought, No, please, this can't be happening. I'm getting married today! But I'm used to dealing with last-minute problems, so I rallied my strength, got my hair and makeup done, got into my gown and veil, and went off to the church to get married.

Left to right: My father, Frederick Fulcher, my maid of honour BJ Talbot, me, my bridesmaid Ollie Mark, and my mother, Muriel Fulcher

I was worried about my dad walking me down the aisle because he might be nervous. I had assured him it was just a small little church with a short aisle — Newman Centre Chapel. Then something strange happened. As we stepped into the chapel, I started to shake. I couldn't stop. I had never had such a case of nerves in my life! My dad, would you believe, was perfectly calm.

Added to this, I had this terrible cold. I had Kleenex stuffed everywhere. We got to the altar and my dad started to hand Bruno the ring, and I got a coughing fit. The priest, Father Stone, looked at me and said, "Eleanor, do you want me to stop for a while?"

"No…[cough, cough]….no — I'll be all right…. Dad, give Bruno the ring…" My dad was nearby with the tissues and I'm coughing away. It was awful. I was a wreck, a total wreck. Somehow I made it through the ceremony.

We had our reception at Fran's restaurant at Yonge and St. Clair. We had about 150 guests. Fran's was a Toronto institution. Bruno had done a recent renovation job at this location for the owner, Fran Deck, and Fran was so grateful that he told Bruno, "I want to give you the reception here — food and all. It's my wedding present to you." Well, what could be better? We had no money; we were just starting out. I had just launched my business and Bruno had just started his business, so we were really strapped financially. This generous gift was huge, huge! We had a wonderful reception — though not without incident.

The food was lovely. It was the first party they'd had in this new reception room Bruno had designed and renovated and everything was great — ice sculptures, decorations, and a band. But someone

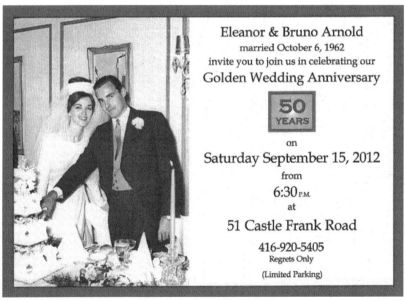

Bruno and I celebrated our 50th wedding anniversary in 2012

didn't deliver the wine or the soft drinks as ordered. All they had at the time were vodka and rye, so the bartender decided to mix martinis and Manhattans while waiting for the other beverages to be delivered. (I later discovered that Bruno had planned the whole thing!) These cocktails were presented on trays as the guests arrived. All my relatives were there, many of whom didn't drink at all. (My mother and some of my aunts weren't speaking to each other and my mother had said, "Eleanor, if you invite so and so, I'm not coming." But I was firm. "It's my wedding and I get to choose the guests.")

So there we were all together, friends, relatives, loved ones and not-so-loved ones. Everyone, including me, accepted these drinks that were in lovely stemmed glasses, probably thinking it was fruit juice. Well, within half an hour you've never seen so many tipsy guests in your life. It was hilarious. Everyone was everyone's best friend — all talking and laughing and dancing and hugging. It was so funny and so perfect. And quite amazingly, I forgot all about my cold!

In addition to *my* family, we had guests from Switzerland — Bruno's father and his new bride. Bruno's mother had died several years before. His father had later taken up with a waitress that he'd met in a tavern in Switzerland. Bruno's father was a top architect in his canton and this young waitress was quite smitten. Eventually it came to my attention that Bruno's two brothers and their wives were not happy with this situation. They thought it highly inappropriate at his age. They decided that they would find him a suitable partner — and they did. They found Rosa, a delightful, "age-appropriate" widow.

As the date of our wedding approached, one of Bruno's brothers called to announce that their father and Rosa were getting married. "Wouldn't it be wonderful if they came to Canada to attend your wedding on their honeymoon?" Um, okay, we thought, we guess so. Bad decision.

Bruno went to Montreal the day before our wedding to pick them up, and little by little, our special time seemed to be revolving more and more around his dad and Rosa, not us. To the point where, after the wedding, all four of us flew to New York together. Bruno and I were spending a few days there for our honeymoon and his dad and Rosa were catching a cruise out of New York.

Neither Bruno's father nor his new wife spoke English and soon I was ready to scream because Bruno had to keep translating and his focus was on them, them, them. They were leaving early the next morning for their cruise so I told myself, Eleanor, you can hang in there for one more day. So in the morning we got them all packed and ready to go, and we got them down to the docks to see them off. And there's no boat — no people — no cars. What...?

Bruno's father had read the tickets wrong. The boat wasn't leaving until 8 o'clock that night, not 8 o'clock in the morning.

I just cracked. I thought, I cannot handle this. Bruno took me aside and said, "We have to do this, we have to. We'll take them on a city tour and then they'll be off, and we'll go out tonight and celebrate." Fine. We got through the day, and they finally boarded the ship and sailed off. Bruno and I went to the Waldorf Astoria for our big night. Alone at last. As we were having dinner, Gordon McCrae, the headliner, came over to our table and sang the song Bruno had requested, "All the Way," which is our song. Finally, finally, we were starting our honeymoon. But suddenly I was so overwhelmed with pent-up emotions that the dam burst. I started bawling. I couldn't help it and I couldn't stop. Gordon McCrae didn't know what to do. The whole room was focused on our table. He tried patting me on the back while still singing, which only made it worse.

After that very public breakdown, the honeymoon was perfect.

A year later, 1963, we had a second honeymoon of sorts when we went to Switzerland. I met the rest of Bruno's family. I remember being at a church service and was struck by the fact that all the men sat on one side and all the women sat on the other. But I didn't notice this until the service was over and I realized I'd been sitting with all the men! On that same trip, Bruno and I picked up our brand new Fiat, which we were having shipped back to Canada. When we went to the factory to get it, we found the factory was closed every day from 1 p.m. to 3 p.m. for lunch. They have their big meal at lunchtime. A very different culture!

After Bruno and I married, we settled into life in Toronto. It was wonderful. We were both building our businesses, starting to make some money, and had a wonderful social life. We weren't really thinking about having children for a few years. We thought we'd get more settled first. Like you press a button and after two or three years, say Okay, we're ready, boom, press the button, here we go. Well, once we were ready, nothing happened, nothing happened, nothing happened. It got to the point where I'd call and say, "Bruno, you have to come home — *now*. The time is right!" (Where does the romance go?)

Eventually we decided to put our names in for adoption, with the thought that if we got pregnant in the meantime that would be fine too. One year later we adopted our darling daughter Angela when she was three months old. We then proceeded to thoroughly spoil her.

After a year we decided she needed a brother or sister. We called our Catholic Children's Aid counsellor and put our names in to adopt another child. We thought it would take another year, but we got a call one week later! Apparently once you have proven yourselves to be good parents, your name gets moved up on the waiting list and our counsellor had the perfect fit for us. We were thrilled when we learned that we could adopt Marcus. We were able to pick him up right from the hospital when he was one week old. He made our family complete. We love them deeply. What a double blessing.

New dad Bruno with Angela in 1969

The young mother with Angela, left, and Marcus

I read something recently about the adoption process that gladdened my heart. The leader of the Progressive Conservative Party of Ontario, Tim Hudak, said he would reward adoption agencies for finding kids new homes. Yes! In the current system, agencies are funded by the number of children still in their care, so there is no

Bruno and I with Angela and Marcus, 1978

incentive for them to get the children adopted. In the mid-1990s I had a brief experience with our foster care system. I visited a foster family on two occasions and had the opportunity to talk to the foster mother. She was looking after four or five children, all under four years of age. She was a lovely lady, deeply concerned about the government policies regarding adoption. Apparently, in its hope that each child will be reunited with its natural parents, children are kept in foster homes for years in case the parent or parents straighten out.

With Marcus and Angela

Angela at 14

Marcus and my granddaughters Madison (middle)
and Peyton

Meanwhile, 80 percent of the time the natural parents would say
they were coming to visit, and she would get the child bathed and
dressed and looking forward to the visit, and the parents wouldn't
show up. Not even call. Now, how many strikes and you're out?
Many of these children, once they reach a certain age, are not adopt-
able as easily as babies and toddlers. I know from personal acquain-
tances that due to the long waiting list — sometimes years — the
hopeful parents have gone elsewhere. China, for instance, has a
waiting list of just months. And why? For parents who are dead-
beats, in many cases. Yes, give them time if the circumstances allow,

Celebrating my 69ᵗʰ birthday with Bruno, Lori and Marcus

Vittoria at her first model shoot

Joseph attended the Robert Land Academy when he was about 12

but how long? And who decides? In the meantime these poor children are deprived of a permanent, loving home and often end up going from one foster home to another. Is it any wonder some of them grow up with huge problems? We can do better. We must do better! There should not be one child unable to be adopted in Canada. We are a loving, caring people. We can make this happen. You have my vote, Tim Hudak.

I'm grateful that the adoption process worked so well for our family. Bruno and I are now grandparents. Marcus and Lori have two girls. Madison is 10 and Peyton is five and they are doing fine — great kids, as opposite as day and night. Angela, married and divorced, has two wonderful children, Joseph, 22, and Vittoria, 20.

No one could possibly envisage how life changes when you have children. You can't possibly understand how much of your life it will take up — and willingly. You can say goodbye to many of those things you used to do so often — dinner parties, theatre and so on. But it's all worth it.

Fast forward 40 years. Marcus is the president of Bruno's company, Euromart International, of which Bruno is the chairman of the board. It's an international real estate company with a lot of investors from Europe. Bruno shows no signs of slowing down. He looks ten years younger than he is because he takes good care of himself, staying fit with jogging and a healthy diet. He still travels to Europe and elsewhere four or five times a year on business and keeps in close touch with his relatives in Switzerland. Bruno bought a condo in Lugano so we'd have a place to stay when we visit our Swiss relatives and friends.

I've had a wonderful marriage to Bruno — 50 years in 2012! — and I think the secret, for me at least, is that he lets me be me. I don't feel tied down.

The freedom of it! I'm an independent person and Bruno is too. Some men want their wives around all the time and are helpless without them. Thank God Bruno isn't like that. He has a lot of foreign clients, which means lots of travel. When they come to Toronto to talk business, he has to entertain them for the evening. He's not going to leave them alone to fend for themselves in a strange city and

Bruno, 1996

expect to earn their trust and their business. You have to show them around, treat them well. I've been in business. I know it's important and I'm fine with that.

If I had a husband who said every day, "I'll be home at 5 o'clock and we'll have cocktails and then dinner will be at 6 o'clock ..." I'd go insane. We have a good balance in our marriage. I'm busy. I have my own things going on, and I'm glad he does too. The time we have together is very precious. We never take each other for granted.

When Bruno and I got married everyone said it wouldn't last three months (based on my history?) but in 2012 we celebrated our golden anniversary. I've been in an investment group called the Globetrotters for 35 years. We had lunch the other day and I looked around and realized that of the eight of us left, only two aren't widowed. What an awakening. I know I'm one of the lucky ones.

Bruno and I are the same age. He really works at staying healthy because he has no intention of retiring. Many of my friends have lost their husbands who were older than them. My dear friend Cathy

Bruno and me, October, 2012

Richardson lost her husband last year, and even though she has a very busy social life and is always out and doing things, she told me it hits her hardest when she goes home and the house is empty. He's not there. Even though I love that Bruno is independent and still working and travelling, I have to admit I look forward to our evenings together. It's nice when he's around.

The Place We Call Home

I like to tell the story of how Bruno and I bought our first (and only) house on Castle Frank Road in Toronto. Bruno wanted to own a house — I didn't. I loved our small one-bedroom apartment. Besides, we couldn't afford a house. However, we kept looking at properties. It almost became a pastime.

One day he asked me to make an appointment to look at some

new townhouses. I was to meet the builder/owner, Magda Kelner, at her house at 51 Castle Frank Road, which was right across from the new townhouses I was to inspect. When I walked into her house and looked around, I got this wonderful warm feeling. In all sincerity, I looked at her and said, "If you ever think of selling this house, let me know."

And she said, "I just listed it yesterday!"

I said, "I don't want to see the townhouses. I want to call my husband now." I told Bruno I'd found the perfect house (way over our budget) and he must get here fast. When you want something badly enough you fight for it — and we got it. It took five hours of my husband and Magda negotiating, but eventually we all signed a handwritten agreement. Bruno and I gave her a deposit and we all went out to Julie's, one of Toronto's finest restaurants at the time, to celebrate.

The next morning Magda phoned early in the morning to say that there was an offer on her desk for 10 percent more than we had paid!

Bruno and me at our 50th anniversary garden party, 2012. It's a good life. Cheers!

Somehow I had known deep down that we had to act fast, or else. And the hand-written contract held.

We have lived in this house for 45 years. It is always comforting and welcoming. It's home. I think it's wonderful if you have a place that allows you to forget about business, relax, feel protected and stress-free. Yes, it was worth the 25-year mortgage. It was a great incentive to work even harder. And we still love it.

CHAPTER 14

FINDING MYSELF

I get together three or four times a year with The Girls, a group of friends I grew up with. There isn't one of them that isn't smart and bright and totally with it, but I'm the only one who had my own business. All of them married young, at 18, 19 or 20, and have had interesting, happy, fulfilled lives. Sometimes I get the feeling that some wish they'd had more time to go out in the world and do more and see more before they married. But that was then. I had no idea what I wanted when I was 20 years old. How can you know yourself until you go through some life experiences while single? That's how you find yourself and discover who you are — your values, your dreams, your heart.

In the '50s and '60s, as I mentioned, you were considered an "old maid" if you weren't married by the time you were 25. Today the majority of women don't marry until they're 25 or older. Times have changed. Women have more opportunities — education, executive jobs, their own businesses, and money. It's now their choice when and if they want to marry.

I think it's okay to kind of float for a while in your teens and twenties. Take time to eliminate what you don't want. Travel, volunteer, earn a bit of money at various jobs while you clear your head and discover what you really want. When you find your passion, you'll find your voice and your destiny.

Don't depend on someone else for your happiness in life. Even having Bruno and my family and my dear friends, I've never relied on anyone to provide me with happiness. That's my responsibility. I go out and get it! I've learned what makes me happy and brings me joy, and I've always made sure to indulge in those things at least twice a week, whether it's getting together with friends, a concert, a nice dinner at a favourite restaurant, or any number of things that I enjoy. Do treat yourself well!

When my granddaughter Vittoria turned 16, I arranged a professional modelling photo shoot for her. She's tall, slim and beautiful. Traute Siebert loved her, and we could have opened many doors. But she said, "Nana, I don't know, I'm not too sure." It wasn't her time; it wasn't her thing. Later, she told me she didn't have the confidence or interest to do what we expected, even with me there beside her all the way. If she'd really wanted it, I would have been there for her however long it took.

Three years later Vittoria did find her passion — dog grooming, and she's great at it! Life is full of surprises.

So find your passion. Then follow it with all your heart. Once you do that, it's surprising how the rest of it falls into place and you find yourself a happy and fulfilled person.

Along the way, dance, sing, get out there with people and enjoy life. Look after yourself and keep well.

And above all, be ready for anything!

POSTSCRIPT

I must apologize for having taken so long to write this book. The fact is, it is my third attempt. The first, in 1985, was written in collaboration with Frank Rasky and was called *Models and Movie Stars*. It never got finished due to business conflicts, although it was nearly completed. For the second effort I took a totally different approach. The book was going to be 80 percent pictures and 20 percent story — after all, I did have the largest fashion and beauty archives in Canada, with photos spanning decades. The collection was a priceless piece of history and an embodiment of my life's work, and would have made a wonderful book. But as I mentioned in Chapter 6, those archives were "thrown out," "ditched," destroyed by a man the police and insurance company could never find. I felt my life had been thrown away. It was only in 2011, ten years after that happened, that I knew — for my own peace of mind and sanity — that I had to write this book. So instead of my now-extinct picture library being published, I have written this book so that this particular period will not be forgotten. I gathered whatever pictures I could beg, borrow or unearth.

But the stories are still there and true and important as a record of those incredible years. What a time it was.

I hope you enjoyed it.

A special thanks to Jennifer Campbell of Heritage Memoirs, whose endless patience during this two-year project has been critical to its completion. Would you believe about 20 manuscript revisions plus trying to organize hundreds of photos, many dog-eared and without names or dates? She's been amazing.

Manufactured by Amazon.ca
Bolton, ON

24865297R00164